GUIDE TO FURNITURE REFINISHING AND ANTIQUING

McGraw-Hill Paperbacks
Home Improvement Series

GUIDE TO FURNITURE REFINISHING AND ANTIQUING

McGraw-Hill Book Company

New York   St. Louis   San Francisco   Auckland   Bogotá   Düsseldorf
Johannesburg   London   Madrid   Mexico   Montreal   New Delhi   Panama
Paris   São Paulo   Singapore   Sydney   Tokyo   Toronto

1 2 3 4 5 6 7 8 9 0 SMSM 8 3 2 1 0

Library of Congress Cataloging in Publication Data

Main entry under title:

Guide to furniture refinishing and antiquing.

   (McGraw-Hill paperbacks home improvement series)
   Originally published in 1975 by Minnesota Mining and Manufacturing
Company, Automotive-Hardware Trades Division, St. Paul, in the Home
pro antiquing guide.
   1. Furniture finishing. 2. Design, Decorative. I. Minnesota Mining and
Manufacturing Company. Automotive-Hardware Trades Division. Home
pro furniture refinishing and antiquing guide. II. Title: Antiquing.
TT199.4.G84 1980 684.1'0443 79-26818
ISBN 0-07-045973-8

Cover photo courtesy of Red Devil Paints & Chemicals, Mount Vernon, New York

Contents ▬▬▬▬▬▬▬

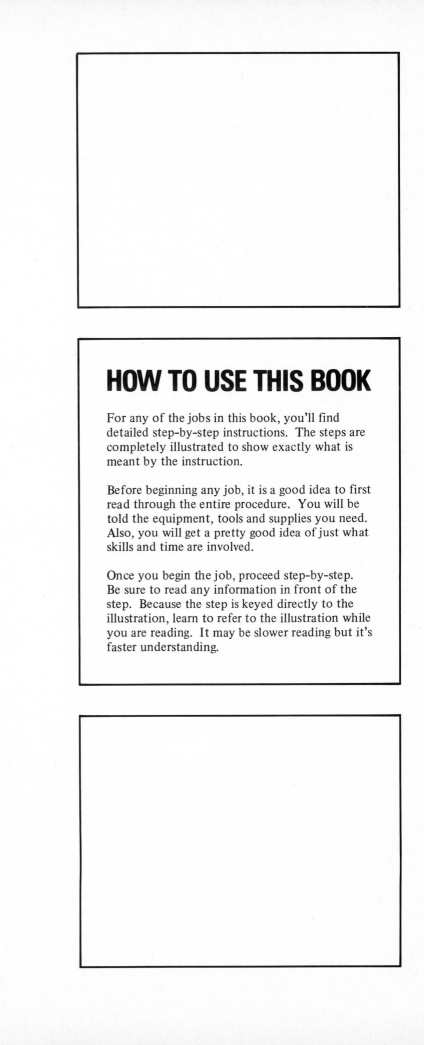

HOW TO USE THIS BOOK

For any of the jobs in this book, you'll find detailed step-by-step instructions. The steps are completely illustrated to show exactly what is meant by the instruction.

Before beginning any job, it is a good idea to first read through the entire procedure. You will be told the equipment, tools and supplies you need. Also, you will get a pretty good idea of just what skills and time are involved.

Once you begin the job, proceed step-by-step. Be sure to read any information in front of the step. Because the step is keyed directly to the illustration, learn to refer to the illustration while you are reading. It may be slower reading but it's faster understanding.

GUIDE TO FURNITURE REFINISHING AND ANTIQUING

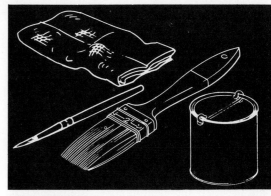

REFINISHING

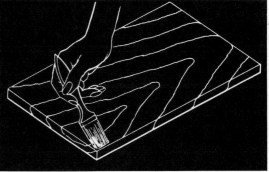

No two refinishing projects are exactly alike. The differences in the wood, the type and amount of old finish, and the amount of repair work required dictate the methods that should be used. The type of finish desired will also determine methods used and final appearance.

Of all the home improvement products on the market today, probably none change as rapidly as paint products and painting tools. Manufacturers are constantly introducing new materials that are longer wearing, easier to apply, and better appearing than last year's products.

For the most current information and best advice available, consult your paint dealer before undertaking any refinishing project. Most paint retailers are very knowledgeable about their products.

After selecting a product, be sure to read the label concerning the manufacturer's cautions, instructions and recommendations regarding their product, the surface preparation and the method of application. This is very important as some products with similar names have different contents and uses.

Always be sure that the products you purchase are compatible with each other. For example, after staining an item, you should use a finish of the same brand or at least one recommended by the manufacturer of the stain. This practice will ensure that each surface coating is the best possible combination for long wear and appearance.

■■■ PREPARING THE SURFACE ■

This section describes the procedures that should be followed to properly prepare a wood surface before applying a stain or finish coat.

In some cases you may want to remove the old finish before applying a new finish. The main reason for removing the old finish is to provide a clean bare surface for applying a clear finish. If you are applying a colored finish, you do not need to remove the old finish unless there is an excessive build-up of many layers of old finish.

Minor repairs are often needed to prepare the surface for finishing. Some of the more common repairs that may be required are described in this section.

After the surface has been repaired, it is ready to be sanded. Sanding is one of the most important steps in getting a quality finish. The finish can only be as smooth as the surface it goes on. It is impossible to achieve a good finish over a poor sanding job. The various types of abrasive paper, their grit size and the proper methods for sanding are included in this section.

The last part of this section contains the proper method for applying a modern two-step bleach. If you desire a natural or clear finish which shows the wood grain, you may have to change the color of the raw wood by bleaching it.

▶ **Removing Old Finish**

Removing an old finish is a messy job. If the old finish must be removed, and you prefer not to do it, there are professional furniture refinishers who can do this job for you. However, with readily available chemical paint removers, the home pro can easily do the job himself. This section provides the procedures to achieve professional results.

A commercial paint remover is a much more efficient way to remove the old finish down to bare wood than sanding or other mechanical means. Paint removers contain a mixture of various chemicals which soften the old finish. It can then be removed by gentle scraping or it can be washed away with water, depending on type of remover used. Paint removers or varnish removers may be used, as there is no difference between the two. They are available in a liquid or semi-paste form.

Removing Old Finish

Most paint removers include a paraffin wax that coats the surface and must be removed with solvent such as paint thinner. Some of the other removers contain a different type of wax that does not remain on the surface. These are often called "no clean-up" removers. However, they may not leave the surface entirely wax-free. If this is the case, you will have to sand the surface lightly to remove any residue and reach the bare wood.

Some of the better removers you find on the market today are washable types. The chemicals and waxes in the remover combine with water and are simply rinsed from the surface. If the procedures are followed carefully, the surface is clean and bare.

The major advantage of washable removers is the speed, efficiency, and simplicity of water wash-up.

Unless you are working on a surface with delicate veneers and old glues that may loosen when water is applied, the simplest method is to use the washable type of remover. If you are working on a large surface, with cost of materials a factor, use a less expensive remover to take off most of the old finish. Then complete the job with an application of the washable type.

PREPARING THE SURFACE

Removing Old Finish

When applying paint remover to a stationary
vertical surface, a semi-paste remover should be
used. This type holds to vertical surfaces better
than liquid types. When working with semi-paste
removers, keep in mind that as the old finish
softens, the remover becomes more liquid. So be
prepared for some runoff and reapply remover as
needed to keep the surface covered.

There may be cases when you will need to use a
bleach after removing the finish. Some removers
tend to discolor lighter wood or transfer bright
colors of paint into the wood. Bleaching would
be needed to remove the coloring. Bleaching may
also be required if the surface below the old finish
has been stained. The remover may or may not
take off the stain along with the finish. The same
situation is true if stained filler has been used on
coarse-grained woods such as walnut or mahogany.

The water-washable-type remover takes off more
stain and filler than most other removers. If
unwanted coloring remains, try a quick wash with
bleach. Remember, however, that bleaches will
also lighten the color of the wood while removing
the stain. Go to Page 25 for information regarding the use of wood bleaches.

Removing Old Finish

With some jobs, there may not be a need to
remove the finish from all areas, such as the inside
of a drawer or cabinet, sides of shelving, backs of
doors, etc. If remover does get on these areas,
they may be damaged enough so that complete
finish removal may be required.

Use masking tape [1] and masking paper or news-
paper to keep remover off areas that do not
require finish removal. Also, apply remover no
closer than about a quarter inch from edges of
these surfaces. Then complete removal of old
finish by sanding.

Be sure to read the following section on preparing
a surface before starting to refinish a piece of
furniture. This will enable you to purchase or
gather all tools and materials needed and to plan
your job.

Removing Old Finish

Most old finishes can be removed by using a paint remover. The following tools and supplies are required:

Paintbrush [1]. Use brush with a wooden handle and natural bristles. A plastic handle and synthetic bristles may be softened or dissolved by the remover.

Rubber scraper [2]. Used to take off paint remover from indented or curved surfaces.

Stiff-bristle brush [3]. Used to take off remover from carved areas.

Wide-blade putty knife [4], if required. Extra fine grade finishing pads or steel wool grade 00. Can be used instead of a scraper to take off remover from curved areas.

Rubber gloves. Wear these if you think your hands will come in contact with the remover.

Paint remover

Old rags or paper towels

Removing Old Finish

Be sure to read the following WARNING before attempting to remove old finish. Also, carefully read the label on the can of paint remover that you have purchased.

WARNING

Most paint removers are poisonous. Keep them out of reach of children and pets. Wash skin thoroughly after using.

Use paint remover only in an area with adequate ventilation. Avoid breathing vapor and contact with skin or eyes.

Avoid storing paint remover. Buy only enough for each job. Excessive pressure may build up in the container. When this happens, the contents may be sprayed out when the container is opened.

Some paint removers labeled nonflammable may still ignite under certain conditions such as after being spread on a surface. Be sure to keep any item away from open flames until all remover has been taken off.

PREPARING THE SURFACE

Removing Old Finish

If the weather permits, plan to complete all stripping of old finish out of doors. Otherwise, use the garage or basement with windows or doors open.

1. Select location. Spread newspapers down. Place the item on the papers.

Whenever possible, apply paint remover to a horizontal surface to prevent runoff. It may be necessary to turn the item several times.

2. Place item in desired position.

WARNING

If paint remover has been in warm temperatures with tightly sealed cap, a cloth should be placed over the cap when opening. This will prevent the contents from spraying when opened.

3. With cap pointing away from you, carefully loosen cap. Remove cap.

Removing Old Finish

Always spread a full, thick layer of paint remover on the surface. Do not rebrush. Use one full stroke only.

4. Pour a full, thick layer of paint remover [1] on surface. Spread evenly with full brush strokes.

5. Check surface for thin or dull spots.

If there are thin or dull spots, apply additional paint remover to these areas.

6. Allow time for softening of old finish as indicated by manufacturer's instructions on label of paint remover.

7. Press finger into old finish [2] with small circular motion. Check that old finish has softened.

If old finish has softened, go to Page 7 (top) if using water-washable remover. Go to Page 7 (bottom) if using "no clean-up" remover.

If old finish has not softened, the remover may have evaporated before it penetrated the old finish. Perform Step 8.

8. Using a wide-blade putty knife, remove as much softened finish [3] as possible. Repeat Steps 4 through 7.

1

2

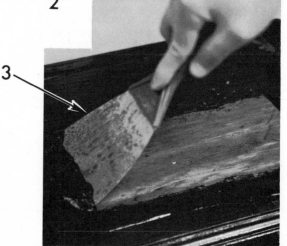

3

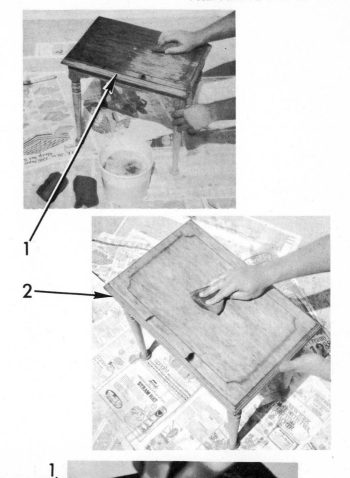

Removing Old Finish

Always loosen old finish by rubbing with the grain.

9. Using finishing pad or steel wool and bucket of water, gently scrub old finish [1].

A bristle brush and steel wool should be used to remove the loosened finish from uneven surfaces such as grooves and intricately carved areas.

10. Continue to loosen and remove finish with finishing pad or steel wool and water.

11. Using old rags or paper towels, wipe off as much water from item [2] as possible. Go to Step 16, Page 8.

Removing Old Finish

Always remove old finish by scraping wood with the grain.

12. Using putty knife, scrape off as much loosened finish [1] as possible.

After most of the finish has been removed with putty knife, finishing pad or steel wool or bristle brush should be used to remove the finish from grooves and carved areas.

13. Continue removing finish [2] with finishing pad or steel wool or bristle brush.

14. Using warm water and finishing pad or steel wool, scrub off remaining paint remover.

15. Using old rags or paper towels, wipe off as much water as possible from item [3].

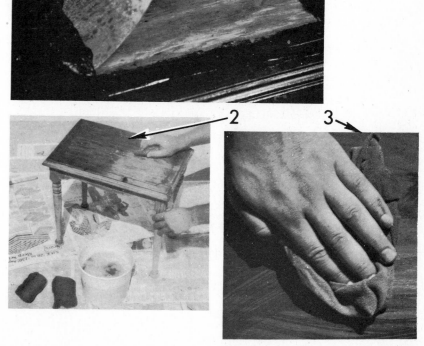

Removing Old Finish

16.   Allow surface to dry completely before
      continuing.

After the surface has dried completely, there may
be small areas of old finish [1] remaining. Do not
reapply the paint remover. These areas can be
easily removed by sanding, since the paint has
been weakened by the remover.

17.   Check the surface for cracks, dents or
      scratches.

If surface is free of defects, go to Page 18 for
sanding procedures.

If surface has minor defects, go to next section
(below) for minor repair procedures.

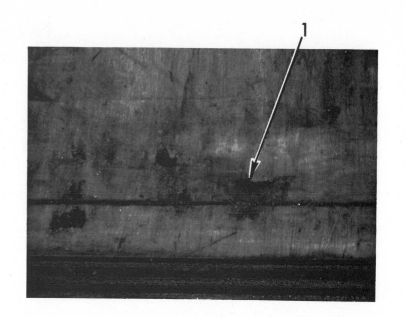

▶ **Minor Repairs**

After removing the old finish, the next step is to
prepare the surface for sanding. It is best to make
all repairs before sanding since many repairs
require sanding after they are completed.

Your first step in making repairs is to determine
what defect you actually have. Then go to the
appropriate page as indicated below.

Removing Surface Blemishes, Page 9.

Removing Dents, Page 12.

Repairing Holes and Cracks, Page 13.

Repairing Damaged Veneer, Page 14.

Regluing Joints, Page 16.

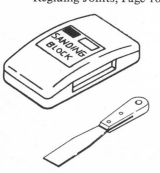

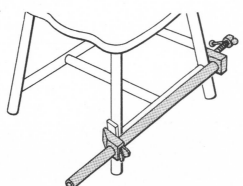

▶ **Removing Surface Blemishes**

Often old ink marks or dark stains embedded in the wood grain should be left untouched. Some of these marks add character to an item, giving it interesting decorative effects.

Other stains and burn marks, if removed, may leave the wood grain a lighter color than surrounding area. The entire surface will then have to be shaded in an effort to blend the two grain colors.

However, too much sanding will reduce richness of color and change the texture of the surface. So carefully examine the blemish and determine if it requires removal.

There are different methods to use depending on type of blemish. Removal procedures for different types of blemishes are listed below. Below each type are the tools and supplies that are required to remove the blemish.

Removing Surface Blemishes

Removing Dark Rings or Spots begins on Page 10. You will need:

    Oxalic acid, 1 ounce powdered or 2 ounces of crystals
    Ammonia, 1 tablespoon
    Paintbrush or clean cloth

Removing Ink Marks begins on Page 11. You will need:

    Ammonia
    Small brush
    Clean cloth

Removing Grease Spots begins on Page 11. You will need:

    Mineral spirits or common dry cleaning fluid
    Small brush
    Clean cloth

Removing Vegetable Oil Spots begins on Page 11. You will need:

    Acetone
    Small brush
    Clean cloth

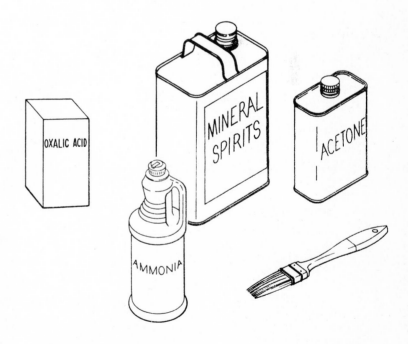

Removing Burns begins on Page 11. You will need:

    Knife
    Sandpaper, Grade 100 medium

▶ **Removing Surface Blemishes — Dark Rings or Spots**

Oxalic acid or common household bleach may be used to bleach dark rings and spots out of wood surfaces. Follow procedures below for mixing and application.

1. Mix the oxalic acid powder or crystals into one pint of hot water.

Oxalic acid mixture may also bleach the natural wood color when removing rings or spots. You should apply the mixture over entire surface to get a uniform color.

2. Using a brush or cloth, apply mixture to entire surface [1].

Dark rings [2] should slowly disappear after mixture has soaked into surface.

If spots or rings do not disappear as desired, repeat Step 2.

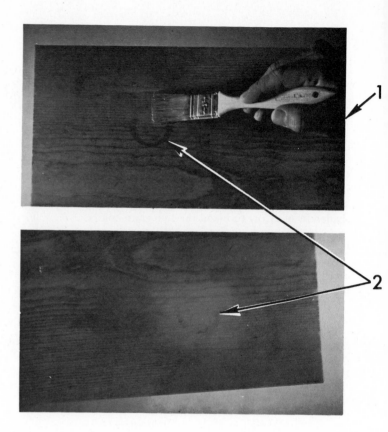

Removing Surface Blemishes — Dark Rings or Spots

A solution of ammonia and water is used to rinse oxalic acid mixture from the surface.

3. Mix one tablespoon ammonia with one quart of water.

4. Using ammonia mixture, rinse oxalic acid mixture from surface [1].

5. Using clean water, rinse ammonia mixture from surface. Allow surface to dry for 24 hours.

If spots or rings reappear after surface has dried, surface should be bleached. See Page 25 for bleaching instructions.

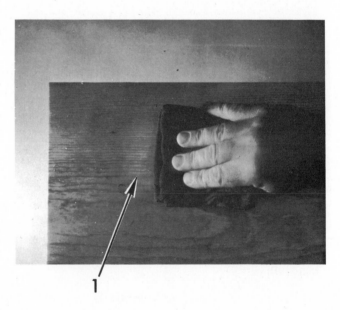

▶ **Removing Surface Blemishes — Ink Marks**

Ammonia is used to remove ink stains from wood surfaces. For proper application, go to Step 1, below.

▶ **Removing Surface Blemishes — Grease Spots**

Mineral spirits, or common household dry cleaner, is used to remove grease spots from wood surfaces. Do not use solvents or paint thinners. For proper application of mineral spirits, go to Step 1, below.

▶ **Removing Surface Blemishes — Vegetable Oil Spots**

Acetone is used to remove vegetable oil spots from wood surfaces. For proper application of acetone, go to Step 1.

1. Using small brush, apply proper solution directly on mark [1] or spot. Using clean cloth, soak up solution.

2. Repeat Step 1 until all marks are removed.

If marks or spots remain after several applications of proper solution, go to Page 10, Step 1 to apply oxalic acid mixture.

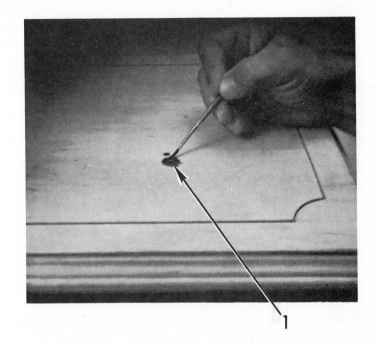

▶ **Removing Surface Blemishes — Burns**

The best way to remove burn marks from surface is to remove all loose, charred particles and then lightly sand entire damaged surface.

1. Using a knife, carefully remove all loose charred particles [1]. Do not cut. Scrape the particles away.

2. Using grade 100 sandpaper, sand damaged area until all burn marks [2] have disappeared.

3. Using grade 100 sandpaper, blend area around mark until surface is as even and smooth as possible.

PREPARING THE SURFACE

▶ **Removing Dents**

When a wood surface is struck by a hard object, the result is either a hole or a dent. A hole [1] results when the wood grain or fibers are cut or removed. For procedures on filling holes, go to Page 13.

A dent [2] results when the fibers are bent. Dents can often be removed by returning the fibers to their original position. This is done by applying steam to the dented area.

If dent is in a surface which is to be painted, follow the procedures on Page 13, Repairing Holes and Cracks.

The following tools and supplies are required to remove dents:

    Iron [3]
    Clean cloth

CAUTION

Wood surfaces may be damaged if too much steam or heat is applied. Some veneered surfaces are held with water-soluble glues. Veneer may be loosened by too much steam.

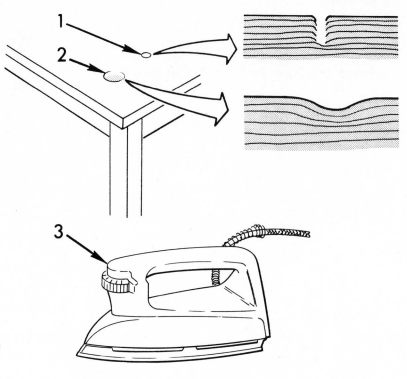

Removing Dents

Steam can be forced into hardwood (oak, maple, walnut) faster if several pin holes 1/8-inch to 1/4-inch deep are first made in dent.

1.   Place damp cloth [2] on dent [1].

CAUTION

Be sure to remove hot iron from cloth when cloth begins to dry.

2.   Place hot iron on cloth [2] until cloth begins to dry.

3.   Remove iron. Remove cloth.

4.   Check that surface has not been damaged by steam.

5.   Check that dent [1] is removed by feeling surface with fingers.

If dent [1] is not removed, repeat Steps 1 through 5.

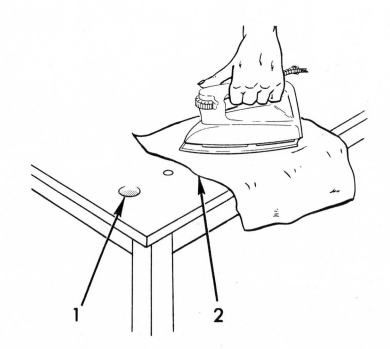

▶ **Repairing Holes and Cracks**

If repairing holes or cracks in a surface which is to be painted with a colored finish or antiqued, go to Page 14.

If repairing holes in a surface which is to be finished with a clear finish, follow the procedures on this page.

The following tools and supplies are required:

Putty knife [1]
Sanding block [2]
Stiff-bristle brush [3]
Sandpaper, Grade 100 medium
Wood putty. Color should be as close as possible to wood being repaired.
Wood stain, if required, to match patched area to color of surface.
Household bleach, if required, to match patched area to color of surface.

1. Using brush, clean dirt from damaged areas.

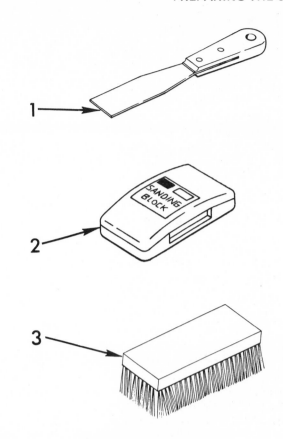

Repairing Holes and Cracks

Be sure to read manufacturer's instructions for correct drying time when using wood fillers.

2. Using putty knife, firmly pack putty into damaged area [1].

3. Allow putty to dry completely before continuing.

4. Using sanding block and sandpaper, sand filled area [2] until it is level with surrounding area.

5. Check color of repaired area with that of surrounding area.

If repaired area is lighter, apply wood stain. Go to Page 31 for information on wood stains.

If area is darker, lighten area with a household bleach. If area remains darker, go to Page 25 for information on bleaching.

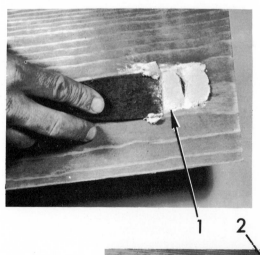

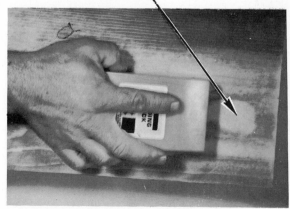

13

PREPARING THE SURFACE

Repairing Holes and Cracks

The following tools and supplies are required to repair holes or cracks in painted surfaces:

> Putty knife [1]
> Sandpaper, Grade 100 medium
> Sanding block [2]
> Dry spackling compound. Dry compound is easy to store and mix as required. Pre-mixed spackling compound is more commonly available. If you do not need large amounts, purchase pre-mixed compound in tubes rather than cans. Cans tend to rust and discolor compound during long period of storage.

1. Mix water with spackling compound until thick paste is formed.

2. Using putty knife, firmly pack paste into hole or crack [3].

3. Allow paste to dry thoroughly according to manufacturer's instructions.

4. Using sanding block and sandpaper, sand repaired area [4] until level with surrounding surface.

5. Paint as desired.

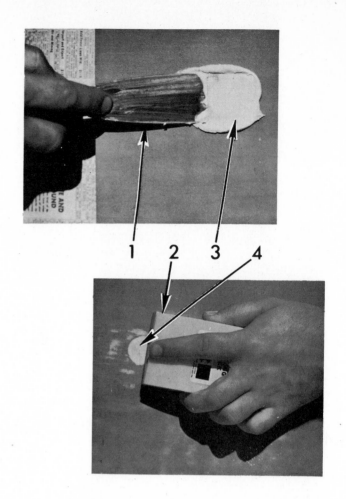

▶ **Repairing Damaged Veneer**

Plywood panels and fine furniture often have a thin (about 1/16-inch) top layer or edging of wood veneer held with glue to a less costly wood. If this veneer is damaged, the damaged section must be replaced. It cannot be repaired. Follow these procedures to patch veneer surfaces.

The following tools and supplies will be required to repair broken veneer:

> Jack knife [1]. A small wood chisel can be used for large areas of broken veneer.
> Sharp knife [2] or single-edged razor blades
> Clamp [3] or, if patched veneer can be positioned horizontally, heavy weights.
> Piece of veneer [4]
> White glue
> Clean cloth or paper towels
> Aluminum foil or plastic wrap

For a good match with damaged area of veneer, try to locate and cut patch from an area of the item where it will not be noticed. If this is not practical, purchase a new piece of veneer that has the same wood grain and matches the color. Slightly dampen the new veneer. Usually this will be its color when it has been finished.

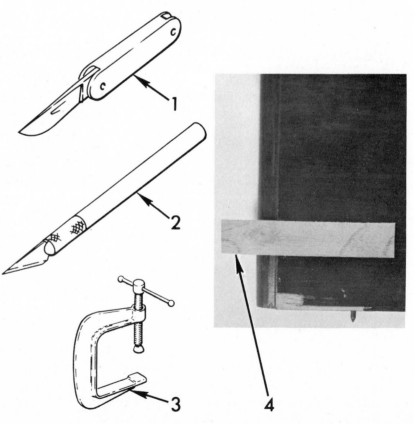

Repairing Damaged Veneer.

1. Measure approximate length and width of damaged area.

An irregular or oblong-shaped patch is less noticeable than regular circle- or square-shaped patches.

A cardboard template may be used to help shape patch.

2. Cutting with the grain as much as possible, cut out desired patch [1] slightly larger than damaged area.

3. Place and firmly hold patch over damaged area [2]. Using knife, mark around patch. Lift patch.

4. Cut along outline until cut is completely through damaged veneer [3].

5. Using knife or small chisel, carefully remove damaged veneer [4] within outline.

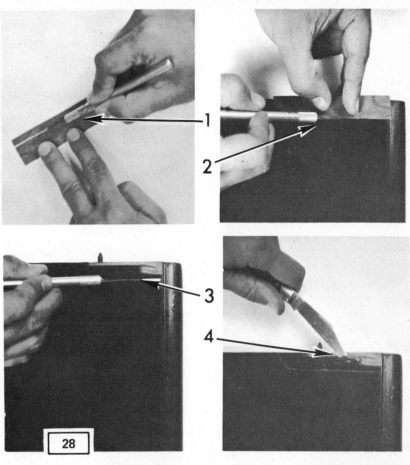

Repairing Damaged Veneer

6. Place patch in outlined area of veneer. Check for exact fit of patch.

If patch is too large, carefully trim patch to correct size.

If patch is too small, go back to Step 1 (above) to cut a new patch.

Glue used to secure veneer on older furniture can be removed by using a cloth moistened with hot water. Newer veneer glue must be scraped off with small chisel or knife.

7. Remove old glue from outlined area [1]. Be sure to remove all of the glue.

8. Apply a light coat of white glue [2] to outlined area and to new patch.

9. Carefully place patch [3] into position on surface.

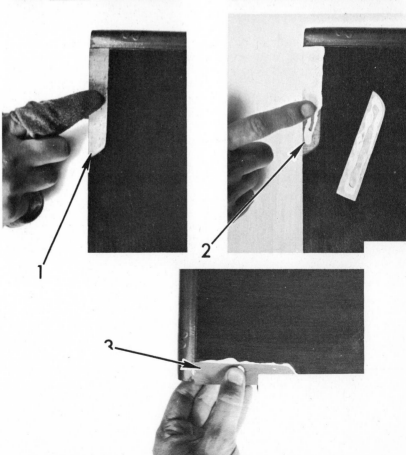

PREPARING THE SURFACE

Repairing Damaged Veneer

CAUTION

Be sure all excess glue is removed from surface. Surface will resist stain wherever glue is not completely removed.

10. Press down firmly in middle and around edges of patch [1]. Wipe off all excess glue.

11. Place a piece of foil or plastic wrap [2] over patch and surrounding area.

Patch must be held tightly with heavy object or wood clamp. This will ensure that the patch will bond tightly to wood when dry.

12. Clamp or place weight on patch.

13. Allow glue to thoroughly dry.

14. Remove clamp or weight. Refinish item as desired.

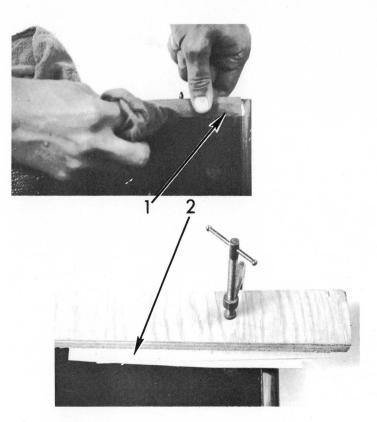

▶ **Regluing Joints**

It is possible for furniture to separate at any joint due to age, weather, or rough handling.

Most joints are made by gluing two sections together. Loosened or separated joints must be reglued to produce a sound piece of furniture.

There are several different methods of repairing loose joints. The method described here is one of the easiest and gives good results. In these procedures, the old glue must be removed and new glue applied to the joints. This applies to both round or square end joints.

The following tools and supplies are required to reglue joints:

> Wood chisel [1]
> Sharp knife [2]
> Claw hammer [3]
> Bar or pipe clamp [4]. Rope tourniquet may be used instead. The length of rope should be long enough to go around item at least three times.
> White glue
> Clean cloth
> Wedges. Small pieces of wood, such as flat toothpicks or wooden matches, are useful.

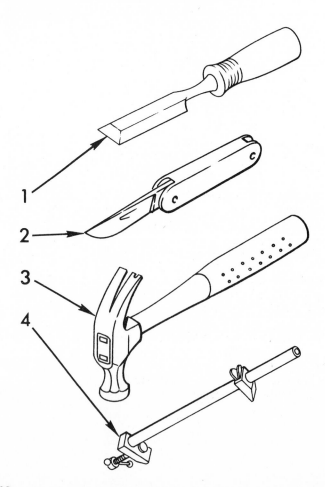

Regluing Joints

White glue will hold joint only if wood is bare and joint is physically tight.

1. Using a chisel or knife, remove all old glue from end [1] and hole [2].

2. Place item on a level surface. This will prevent warping while glue is drying.

3. Apply a coat of white glue to end and hole.

Wood wedges must be forced into hole until end is tightly secured in hole.

4. Place end in hole. Tap wedges [3] into hole around end until end is tight.

5. Using sharp knife, carefully cut wedges even with hole.

CAUTION

Be sure all excess glue is removed from surface. Surface will resist stain wherever glue is not completely removed.

6. Wipe away all excess glue.

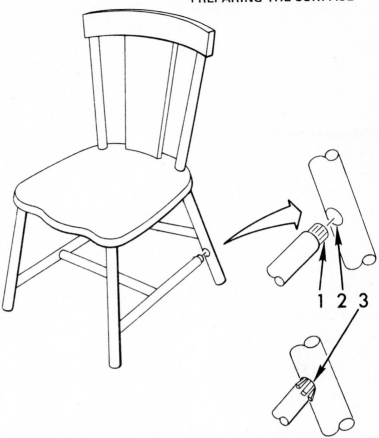

Regluing Joints

Glued joint should be held tightly while glue is drying. If using a rope tourniquet, go to next page for Steps 7-13. If using bar or pipe clamp, continue with Steps 7-9 on this page.

Small scraps of wood should be placed between jaws of clamp and surfaces to prevent damage to surfaces.

7. Using clamp [1], secure joint tightly.

If regluing leg joints, surface above legs should be weighted with books or suitable heavy objects to force leg tightly into joint.

8. Weight down surface, if required. Allow glue to dry thoroughly.

9. Remove clamp. Item is now ready for sanding and refinishing.

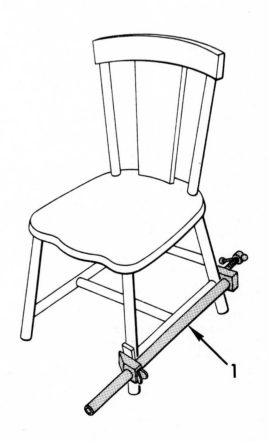

PREPARING THE SURFACE

Regluing Joints

If regluing leg joints, surface above leg should be weighted with books or suitable heavy objects to force leg tightly into joint.

7. Weight down surface, if required.

Steps 8 through 11 describe how to apply a rope tourniquet. Illustrations show some of the different uses.

8. Wrap rope [1] three or four times around legs.

9. Insert stick [2] between bands of rope. Twist stick until most slack is removed from rope.

10. Insert pieces of cloth or cardboard under rope at each leg. This will protect surfaces from damage.

11. Continue to twist stick until rope is tight. Secure stick [3].

12. Allow glue to dry.

13. Remove stick, rope, and pads.

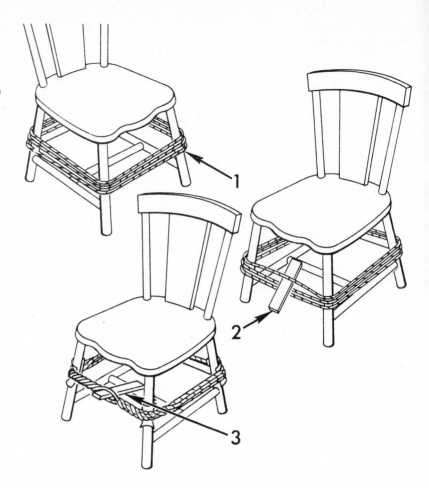

▶ Sanding

After the old paint or varnish has been removed, the surface should be sanded prior to the application of a finishing coat. A good sanding job takes time.

Coated abrasives, frequently referred to as "sandpaper", are most commonly cloth or paper backings coated with minerals of varying types for specific uses. There are five types of coated abrasives in general use:

*   Flint Abrasives — Flint mineral is white in color and most commonly coated on a paper backing for general sanding applications with the major exception of metal.

*   Emery Abrasives — Emery is grey-black in color and commonly coated on a blue cloth backing. Emery abrasives are recommended for removing rust and corrosion from metals.

*   Garnet Abrasives — Garnet products are recognized by their orange-colored mineral and are available both on paper and cloth backings. Garnet is specifically used for wood sanding of all types.

*   Aluminum Oxide Abrasives — This synthetic mineral is brown in color and coated on both paper and cloth backings for broad general application sanding all types of wood and metal.

*   Silicon Carbide Abrasives — Dark black in color. Silicon carbide grain is coated on cloth and paper backings and is recommended for sanding soft woods, plastics, composition materials, paint, varnish, lacquer, etc.

Sanding

Coated abrasive products are available in varying grain or mineral sizes according to two grading systems:

- Retail description – The back of the paper has a word description of the grit size such as FINE, MEDIUM, COARSE.

- Grade numbers – Garnet, Aluminum Oxide, and Silicon Carbide abrasives use this method. Grade numbers range from extra coarse -12 to super fine -600. There are twenty other grade sizes between 12 and 600. However, most refinishing jobs require grades between 50 and 220.

Sanding

The amount of grit covering the backing paper or cloth is called coating. Most abrasive papers are produced in two types – open coating and closed coating.

Open-coat paper has abrasive grains covering about 50% to 70% of the backing. The spaces between the grains help prevent clogging when used on softwoods or painted surfaces. Open-coat paper cuts a little slower than closed-coat paper but does not clog as quickly.

Closed-coat paper has abrasive grains covering the entire backing surface. Closed-coat paper should be used for hardwoods and other surfaces that will not clog the grains quickly.

Sanding may be performed by hand or with the aid of a power sander. Power sanders will do a good job for the initial sanding, but hand sanding is recommended for the final sanding. Keep in mind that too much sanding may destroy the natural richness of color and texture of the wood.

Procedures for hand sanding begin on Page 20.
Procedures for feathering begin on Page 23.
Procedures for power sanding begin on Page 24.

On Page 20 there is a chart describing the grading method, types of paper, and their common uses.

GRADES, MINERALS, AND USES OF COATED ABRASIVES

Grit or Grade Numbers	Mineral Type					Uses
	Flint	Emery	Garnet	Aluminum Oxide	Silicon Carbide	
600					X	Final sanding or polishing operations. Preparation for mirror-like gloss finishes or producing semi-gloss finishes.
500					X	
400				X	X	
360				X	X	
320				X	X	Scuffing or intermediate sanding of coats of finishing materials, sealers, etc.
280			X	X	X	
240			X	X	X	
220			X	X	X	
180		Fine	X	X	X	Light stock removal; final sanding prior to application of fillers, stain, etc.
150			X	X	X	
120	Fine		X	X	X	
100		Medium Coarse	X	X	X	Medium stock removal; progressing from coarser scratch of initial sanding to a finer scratch.
80	Medium		X	X	X	
60			X	X	X	
50	Coarse	Extra Coarse	X	X	X	
40			X	X	X	
36			X	X	X	Heavy stock removal; rough shaping.
30				X	X	
24			X	X	X	
20			X		X	Stripping operations; removal of old finishes.
16				X	X	
12					X	

▶ **Sanding by Hand**

When sanding by hand some form of backing, other than your fingers or hand, should be used. If surface is sanded by holding sandpaper in your fingers, it will cut into the softer areas [1] and ride over hard areas. This results in a wavy surface of hills and valleys.

Using a sanding block will produce a smooth surface. As the sanding block is moved over the surface, the high spots are leveled. This prevents the softer areas [2] from forming valleys.

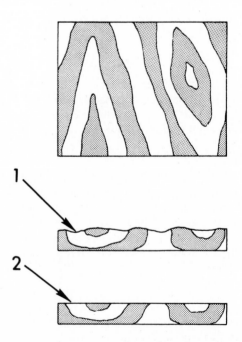

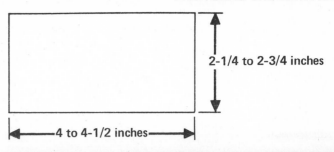

2-1/4 to 2-3/4 inches

4 to 4-1/2 inches

Sanding by Hand

The size of the sanding block depends mainly on your preference. Keep in mind that it is much easier to produce a flat surface with a larger block.

To obtain maximum use of a standard 9-by 11-inch sheet of sandpaper, select a block size that, when covered, is a multiple of the sheet size. The most efficient size of block is about 4 to 4-1/2 inches by 2-1/4 to 2-3/4 inches. This will allow you to get maximum use from a standard sheet of sandpaper.

There are a few good sanding block kits on the market. Some not only include sandpaper cut to size, but the same size paper is available in retail stores. The sandpaper is held in place without use of nails or tacks.

Sanding by Hand

The quality of a finish is a direct result of the care and quality of the preparation of the surface. If you are planning to finish a piece with a clear finish, you should take extra care in sanding the surface. The use of a sanding sealer will enable you to obtain the smoothest possible surface.

When you sand wood, even with fine grades of sandpaper, very small fibers [1] raise up from the surface. These fibers are the broken edges of pores in the wood. As you continue sanding, old fibers are removed, but new fibers are raised because you continue cutting into new pores.

The purpose of sanding sealer is to penetrate and harden the surface. Because the surface is hardened, old fibers are removed but new fibers will not raise up. The sanding sealer turns into a fine powder when sanded and is easy to remove from the surface.

Because sanding sealers penetrate the surface, they may prevent stain from being properly absorbed by the wood. Therefore, always first test the sealer on a hidden part of the furniture or a piece of the same kind of wood.

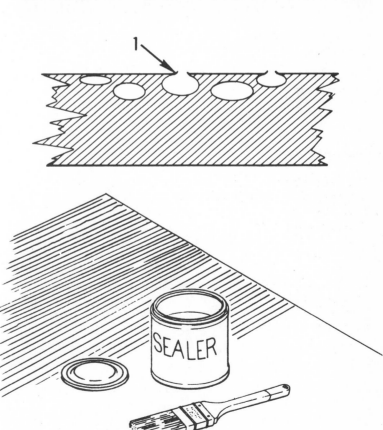

Sanding by Hand

Follow these procedures for best results when sanding by hand.

On some surfaces, better results are often obtained if a sanding block is not used. These surfaces are generally rounded. A block would just sand the higher spots. Instead, use sandpaper with a flexible backing made with cardboard or carpeting. Or simply use several folded sheets of sandpaper.

Some typical surfaces and recommended methods for sanding them are:

- Turned or lathed surfaces — Fold several pieces of sandpaper.

- Rungs or spindles — Use a 2-inch strip of sandpaper.

- Convex curves — Use folded sandpaper backed by a piece of cardboard.

- Outside curves — Use a cardboard tube or a piece of cardboard wrapped with sandpaper.

- Carved surfaces — Use the end of a pencil wrapped with sandpaper.

- When feathering a surface — See Page 23 for feathering technique.

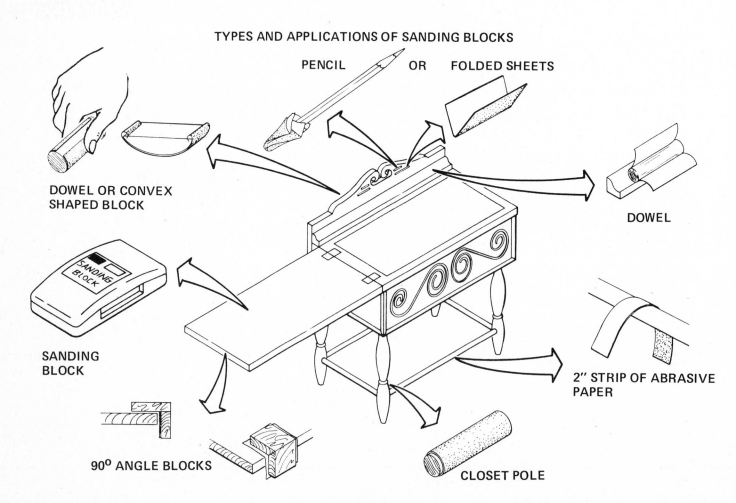

TYPES AND APPLICATIONS OF SANDING BLOCKS

PENCIL   OR   FOLDED SHEETS

DOWEL OR CONVEX SHAPED BLOCK

DOWEL

SANDING BLOCK

2" STRIP OF ABRASIVE PAPER

90° ANGLE BLOCKS

CLOSET POLE

Sanding by Hand

1. Check surfaces to determine methods of sanding to be used.

2. Select sanding blocks or backing as required. See illustration on Page 22.

Always sand surface in the direction of the wood grain, except in the following cases:

- End grain on squared edges [1] — Sand edge squarely.

- Turned or lathed surfaces [2] — Sand in direction of turns.

- End grain on curved edges [3] — Sand with a drawing motion toward you.

3. Using the finest grit that will remove scratches and level the surface, begin sanding.

As soon as surface is level and scratches are not deeper than those produced by the sandpaper, change sandpaper to next finer grit.

4. Continue sanding surface with progressively finer grits until desired surface smoothness is obtained. Use sanding sealer for final sanding, if desired.

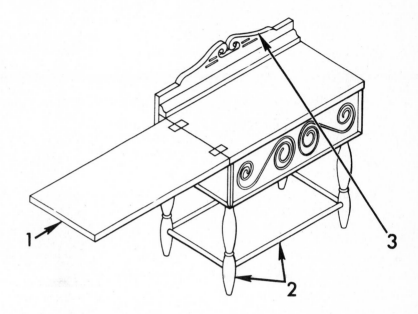

▶ Sanding by Hand — Feathering

Feathering is a sanding technique used to blend the height of a surface with a depression or low spot in that surface. Feathering slopes the surrounding surface gradually into the depression.

By feathering a damaged or repaired area, you can make the area much less noticeable.

Always feather by hand — never use power sanders or sanding blocks. Use a medium-grit sandpaper, about Grade 100 medium.

Begin sanding the edges of the higher surface. Continue gently sanding the higher surface until the edges gradually slope into the low spot [1].

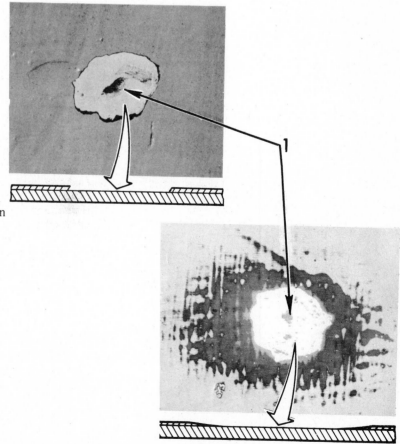

▶ Power Sanding

There are four basic types of power sanders available for small home projects: Vibrating types, both in-line and orbital, the belt type, and the disc sander. The belt and in-line sanders are the only ones that should be used for wood finishing. The other two will produce a circular pattern of scratches on the surface. For additional information on power sanders, see the table (below).

Be sure to always use sanders with the grain. Working across the grain will result in a sweeping or circular pattern of scratches which is difficult to remove.

Use extreme caution when using a belt sander. Belt sanders are fast cutting, even with fine-grit paper, and may burn or gouge the surface. Never use a belt sander on a veneered surface.

SCRATCHES CAUSED BY ORBITAL SANDER

TYPES AND USES OF POWER SANDERS

Types	Disadvantages	Advantages	Application
In-line	1. Slow cutting. 2. Suitable for small jobs. 3. Not recommended for rough sanding.	1. Straight line sanding pattern. 2. Uses standard size abrasive paper. 3. Inexpensive.	1. May be used on veneer surface. 2. May be used for final sanding.
Orbital	1. Produces circular pattern of scratches.	1. Faster cutting than an in-line sander. 2. Inexpensive.	1. May be used on end grain. 2. May be used for smoothing surface to be painted.
Disc	1. Produces swirl pattern of scratches. 2. Hard to control.	1. Fast cutting.	1. May be used on end grain. 2. May be fitted for polishing. 3. Good for metal work.
Belt	1. Fast cutting. 2. Can burn or gouge surface.	1. Straight line sanding pattern.	1. May be used on rough surfaces. 2. May be equipped with polishing belt.

IN-LINE OR ORBITAL

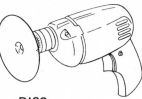

DISC

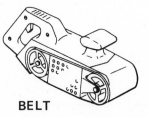

BELT

▶ Bleaching

The process of lightening the color of a wood by use of chemicals is called bleaching. Bleaches remove some or all of the color pigment from the surface wood fibers.

There are two types of bleach most commonly used for wood refinishing:

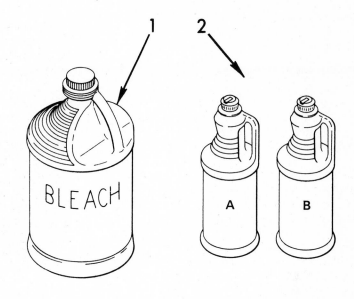

● Household laundry bleach [1] — This bleach is comparatively weak. It is used to slightly lighten the natural wood color and remove stains in a wood surface. It should be used at full strength. Allow it to soak for about 20 minutes. Additional applications will lighten the wood to a similar degree. After bleaching, rinse off with water and wipe dry. Allow surface to dry completely before applying finish.

● Two-step bleach [2] — These bleaches are designed to remove the natural wood color of dark woods, such as mahogany or walnut. The following text gives procedures for applying a common two-step bleach.

Bleaching

The following tools and supplies are required to bleach a wood surface:

> Paintbrushes [1]. Use nylon bristles.
> Two-step bleach [2]
> Extra fine grade finishing pads or steel
>   wool, No. 0000. Used to aid bleach in
>   penetrating surface.
> Sandpaper, Grade 220 extra fine
> Glass containers. Do not use metal con-
>   tainers to hold bleach. They may affect
>   the bleach.
> Protective clothing, rubber gloves, rubber
>   apron, and eyeglasses should be worn.

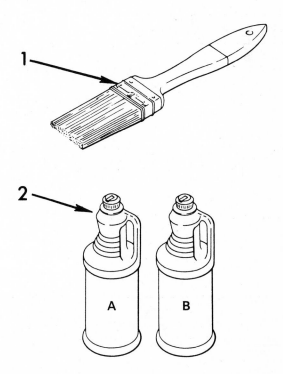

Some types of bleaches require mixing the two solutions just prior to application. Be sure to read manufacturer's instructions before continuing.

Most two-step bleach containers are labeled 1 and 2, or A and B. Be sure to use solution from container marked 1 or A first.

Be sure surface is clean and free of wax. A clean surface enables bleach to work properly and prevents discoloration.

Bleaching

WARNING

Bleach is very strong and caustic. Be sure to wear protective clothing. Read all cautions or warnings on bleach containers.

1. Using paintbrush, apply solution from first bottle freely and evenly to surface [1].

2. Check entire surface for even application. Solution must saturate entire surface and not have dry spots.

If surface has even application and is well saturated, go to Step 5 (below).

If surface does not have even application, spread solution evenly with brush. Go back to Step 2.

If surface is not well saturated, continue.

3. Using finishing pad or steel wool, scrub dry spots to aid penetration of solution.

4. Apply additional solution until surface is well saturated.

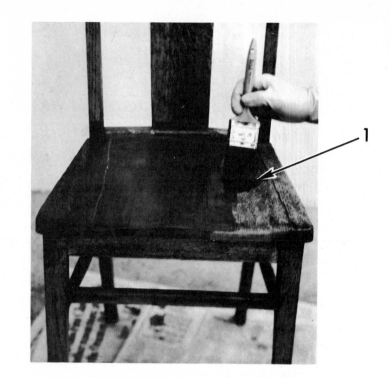

Bleaching

5. Allow first solution to soak into surface for 20 minutes before continuing.

In next step, either a new brush must be used or the brush used with first solution must be thoroughly cleaned.

6. Using a clean brush, apply second·solution freely and evenly to surface [1].

7. Allow second solution to dry. The wood will continue to lighten until surface is completely dry.

8. Check color of surface.

If surface is not at desired lightness, go back to Step 1 (above) for an additional application of bleach.

9. Rinse surface [2] with clean water. Allow surface to dry.

10. Using sandpaper, lightly sand surface to remove any wood grain that may have swelled.

If color is still not at desired lightness, go back to Step 1 (above) for an additional application.

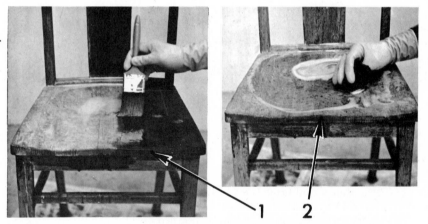

▶ **Description and Use of Sealers**

The main purpose of a sealer is to provide the finish coat with a sound surface to which it will adhere readily.

There are several reasons why a sealer is recommended:

● Sealers prevent stains and undercoating from bleeding into finish coat.

● Sealers harden soft areas of surfaces. Best sanding results are obtained if surfaces are sealed before sanding.

● Sealers allow easier application of wood filler.

Commercial sealers, also called sanding sealers, are compatible with varnished lacquer finishes. Sealers brush on easily and dry quickly. They provide a hard surface. Some sealers also contain a sanding agent which produces a clean, powdery residue without gumming.

Sealers are applied with a brush. Read manufacturer's instructions on the label for drying time and information concerning application because they may differ with different brands.

▶ **Description and Use of Wood Fillers**

In the make-up of wood, there are hundreds of small cells called pores. In some woods, such as oak [1], these pores are very distinct. These woods are called open-grain wood.

In contrast, there are woods, such as pine [2], in which the pores are very small and barely noticeable. These woods are called close-grain wood. There are varying sizes of pores from close- to open-grain woods.

Open-grain wood should be treated with a wood filler to produce an even finish coat. The purpose of a wood filler is to fill the pores and provide a flat surface for the finish. Close-grain woods are usually finished without the use of wood fillers. For types of wood requiring a filler, see the chart on Page 28.

Paste wood fillers are most commonly used. These fillers can be obtained in most of the standard stain colors and also in black, white, or neutral. If in-between colors are desired, a neutral filler and color pigments may be used.

In most cases, wood fillers should be transparent to allow the natural color and beauty of the wood to show.

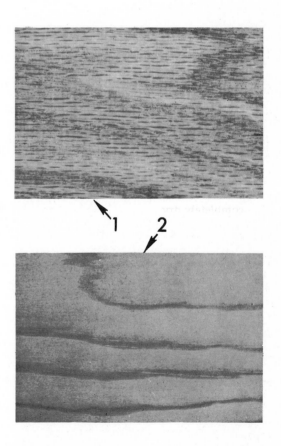

SEALERS AND WOOD FILLERS

▶ **Mixing Wood Fillers**

Paste wood fillers, as purchased, are about the consistency of peanut butter. The filler must be thinned to the proper consistency as shown in the chart (below). The chart shows the amount of thinner required to produce the correct mixture for most of the different types of wood.

Mix only enough filler as needed. After a few hours, filler that has been thinned will dry out and become useless.

The following tools and supplies are required for mixing wood filler:

Putty knife [1]
Paste wood filler
Thinner. Use turpentine for a drying time of 24 to 36 hours. Use naptha for a faster drying time of about 3 to 4 hours.
Two containers. Use one container for mixing filler and one for measuring thinner.

WARNING

Be sure to read manufacturer's cautions concerning breathing of vapor and contact with skin for fillers and thinners.

Procedures for mixing fillers begin on Page 29.

GUIDE FOR THINNING PASTE WOOD FILLER

LIGHT MIXTURE		MEDIUM MIXTURE		HEAVY MIXTURE	
Wood Filler	Thinner	Wood Filler	Thinner	Wood Filler	Thinner
8 ounces	1 pint	8 ounces	10-1/2 ounces	8 ounces	8 ounces
1 pint	2 pints	1 pint	1 pint 5 ounces	1 pint	1 pint
1 quart	2 quarts	1 quart	2 pints 10 ounces	1 quart	1 quart

TYPE OF MIXTURE USED FOR DIFFERENT TYPES OF WOOD

Filler Not Required	Light Mixture	Medium Mixture	Heavy Mixture
Close-Grain Woods —————————————————————▶ Open-Grain Woods			
Basswood	Alder	Butternut	Ash
Cedar	Beech	Mahogany	Chestnut
Cypress	Birch	Rosewood	Elm
Ebony	Cherry	Walnut	Hickory
Fir	Gum		Mahogany (Phil.)
Hemlock	Maple		Oak
Pine	Sycamore		Teak
Poplar			
Redwood			
Spruce			

Mixing Wood Fillers

1. Place correct amount of paste in container. Page 28.

2. Using putty knife, stir paste with folding strokes.

3. Pour correct amount of thinner into separate container. Page 28.

Add a little thinner at a time. This will make mixing easier.

4. Add a small amount of thinner to paste. Stir until thinner blends into the filler.

5. Add increasingly larger amounts of thinner into paste until all thinner is thoroughly blended with filler.

Filler may also be mixed with wood stain to stain and fill in one operation. However, results will not be as good as performing these two steps separately. If desired, you may add penetrating oil stain to the thinned filler until the desired color is obtained. Apply mixture just as you would a filler. The result is a stained and filled surface.

Mixing Wood Fillers

Before applying filler to item being refinished, try a sample on a piece of the same type of wood to determine if filler has been properly prepared.

6. Using procedures described on Page 30, apply sample coat of wood filler.

7. Allow filler to dry, as required.

8. Check for following symptoms of filler and surface and correct as required:

   Pores not completely filled [1] — Filler [2] wiped off too soon. Allow more drying time.

   Small pin holes in filler — Filler was too thin, or was not brushed thoroughly into pores.

   Cloudy surface — Surface was not rubbed enough or rubbing was delayed too long.

9. Go to Page 30 to apply wood fillers.

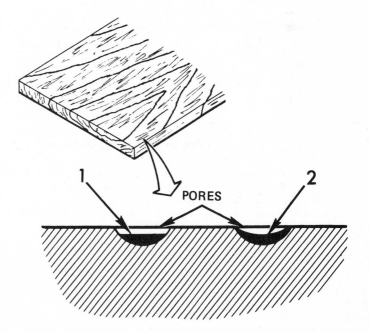

PORES

SEALERS AND WOOD FILLERS

▶ **Applying Wood Fillers**

The following tools and supplies are required for application of wood fillers:

Sanding block [1]   Tack rag
Stiff-bristle paintbrush [2]   Sandpaper, fine grade
Clean cloth, burlap or similar cloth to
    remove excess filler.
Mineral spirits, if required for removal of
    dried filler.

1. Using tack rag, remove all sand dust from pores of surface.

2. Apply a heavy coat of filler on brush. Using brush, rub filler into wood pores with the grain [3] over entire surface.

3. Apply heavy coat of filler to brush. Rub brush across the grain [4] until smooth.

4. Allow filler to set or become dull before continuing.

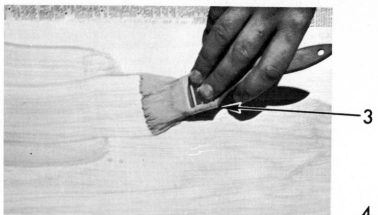

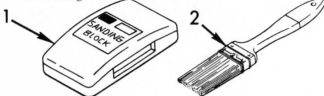

Applying Wood Fillers

In next step, rub across the grain only so that you avoid lifting filler from pores. Be sure to remove all filler from surface to prevent cloudy finish when shellac or varnish is applied.

5. Using cloth, rub across grain to remove filler from surface [1].

If filler has been allowed to harden on surface, apply mineral spirits to cloth and moisten surface. Then use the cloth or a plastic card to remove the filler.

6. Using cloth, rub surface until it is as clean as possible.

7. Check surface for rough or dull spots of wood filler.

If surface is free of spots, go to next page.

If surface has spots, continue.

8. Using sandpaper and sanding block, lightly sand rough or dull spots only [2].

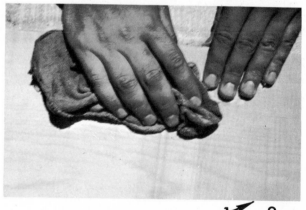

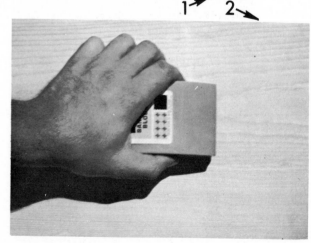

Applying Wood Fillers

Filler should be completely dry before sanding.

Allow 24 to 36 hours drying time if filler was thinned with turpentine.

Allow 3 to 4 hours drying time if filler was thinned with naptha.

9. Using sandpaper and sanding block, lightly sand entire surface.

10. Remove sand dust with tack rag [1].

Surface is now ready for the finish coat.

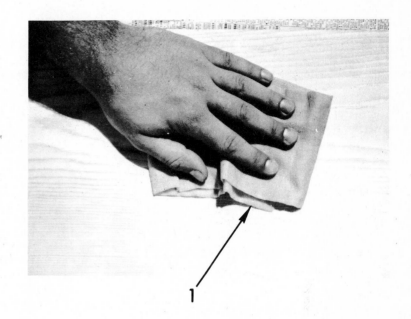

1

WOOD STAINS

▶ Description and Use

A substance that changes the color or tone of wood is called a stain. This change in the wood is caused by a chemical reaction of liquid penetrating the wood fibers and coloring a layer of wood near the surface.

Most wood stains are used to accomplish one or more of the following results:

- Stains are used to make new wood look older.

- Stains aid in matching the natural color of one kind of wood with another.

- Stains add beauty to the natural color of the wood by accentuating the color and grain.

Most of your staining needs may be taken care of by using water stains, non-grain raising stains, or penetrating oil wiping stains.

▶ Water Stains

Water stains are the most inexpensive stains that can be bought. A water stain is an analine dye that dyes the wood fibers just as a cloth would be dyed. The dye tends to penetrate the wood evenly, even when being used on wood of varying areas of open- and close-grain, such as fir plywood.

Stain colors are produced in a complete range of wood tones, plus colors such as red, green, black, etc. These tones and colors may also be diluted with water to obtain a lighter shade.

Water stains are used best on woods that normally require only a slight toning, such as cherry or walnut.

Water stains give wood a clarity and a brillance of color not easily matched by other types of stains.

The main disadvantage of water stains is that they swell the wood fibers and raise the grain. As a result, they make re-sanding necessary. However, with some brands, alcohol as well as water may be used to form a non-grain raising stain.

A second disadvantage of water stains is that the water may loosen glued joints.

Most retail stores do not stock water stains. Therefore, lack of general availability is another disadvantage of these stains.

WOOD STAINS

▶ Non-Grain Raising (NGR) Stains

Like water stains, NGR stains are also an analine dye that will give the wood a similar clarity and brightness. However, these stains have a petroleum by-product base with only a very small amount of water, so they will not cause the wood fibers to swell and the grain to rise.

NGR stains are not recommended for pine, fir, and similar wide-grain woods. The grain pattern will show as wide stripes instead of just being accentuated. Hard close-grained woods, such as oak or maple, respond very well, producing a fairly dark tone.

NGR stains usually dry in about three hours or less, depending on different brands. These stains are available in either mixed or powdered form. Because NGR stains dry quickly, they are very popular among furniture manufacturers. These stains are usually considered an industrial product by most retailers so you may have difficulty obtaining them.

There are numerous common colors of NGR stains but the selection is more limited than other types of stains. The tone of an NGR stain is controlled by thinning the stain with the manufacturer's recommended thinner.

▶ Penetrating Oil Wiping Stains

Penetrating oil wiping stains are made by most paint manufacturers. The procedures in this section describe the use of this type of stain because it is most commonly available. There are several different names for these stains, such as oil stain, pigmented wiping stain, wood stain, or penetrating wiping stain.

Penetrating oil wiping stain leaves most of the color pigment in the pores, cracks, and blemished areas. Leaving most of the pigment in these areas will bring out the grain and blemishes. This is good for creating a "distressed" effect as in antiquing.

Unlike hardwoods such as oak [1], soft and porous woods such as pine [2] tend to soak in a lot of stain. This can darken the wood a great deal. Although penetrating oil wiping stains may be used on all kinds of wood, soft woods that have a wide grain pattern, such as fir or pine, will produce the best results.

Penetrating oil wiping stains are available in all standard wood tones and colors. These stains may also be mixed or diluted with turpentine or mineral spirits to produce lighter tones or to form in-between shades.

UNSTAINED OAK   STAINED OAK

1

2

UNSTAINED PINE   STAINED PINE

They will not raise the grain as water stains do. They do, however, lack the clarity and brightness of water stains.

▶ Selecting a Stain

When selecting a stain color, keep in mind that no two manufacturers produce the same tones. For example, one brand of walnut stain will be different from the color of another brand of walnut stain; one brand of Spanish oak stain may look like another's black walnut. Select a stain from the manufacturer's color chart — not by its name.

When selecting a stain, be sure that it is chemically compatible with the finish that you intend to use. The best way to ensure this is to buy the stain and the finish from the same manufacturer.

Always test a stain by applying it on a hidden piece of the furniture or on a piece of matching wood. Perform all the procedures on the test item. Do them just as you would do them on the actual item being stained. Test for different results (shading, color tones, and darkness) by wiping off the stain quickly [1] or letting it remain for longer periods of time [2].

Also try adding thinner to lighten the color. Then add the finish coat to see how this affects the color and texture. Once the desired results are obtained you are ready to begin the staining job.

▶ Applying Stains

Stains can be applied with a cloth, brush, or spray gun. Most refinishers prefer to use a cloth or brush. Special stain colors and custom mixes should generally be avoided because it is very difficult to achieve the same color each time a new batch is mixed. Always test the stain's color as described above.

Before starting, plan to stain all surfaces in the most convenient sequence:

● First, stain areas that are hidden when the item is in a normal position. Finish the job with areas that are most visible. This will help you avoid having to retouch a previously stained area.

● Divide individual work areas to be stained into groups such as legs, sides, top, etc. Care should be used while applying stain to prevent spilling or splattering stain on other surfaces. Splatter marks will appear as dark spots beneath the finish.

● When applying stains to a large vertical area, always start at the bottom. This allows "sags" or "runs" to be wiped up as you progress. Failure to do this will result in visible dark runs and sag marks.

● When staining a table top, always start at one end and work toward the other end.

● When applying stains to raised or carved areas, carefully wipe high spots so they will be lighter than surrounding areas. This will highlight the raised areas and add to the beauty of the item.

WOOD STAINS

Applying Stains

The entire surface should be stained uniformly. This is easily done on flat, hard surfaces, but is quite difficult to do on soft porous wood or end cuts of wood. Soft wood [1] between grains and porous end cuts [2] will absorb stain almost instantly and become darker than the surrounding areas.

Uniformity can be controlled by using one of two methods described below before applying the stain.

● Apply a very thin coat of shellac to porous areas before applying the stain.

● Apply a thin coat of sealer to porous areas before applying the stain. Go to Page 27 for applying sealers.

Keep in mind that if too much sealer or shellac is applied, the stain will be prevented from being absorbed into the wood. Your objective is to reduce absorption, not prevent it.

For best results, apply two or more thin coats of stain, rather than one heavy coat. The stain should be diluted with the recommended thinner to make it thin enough to apply several light coats. Be sure to allow the preceding coat to dry thoroughly before applying the next coat.

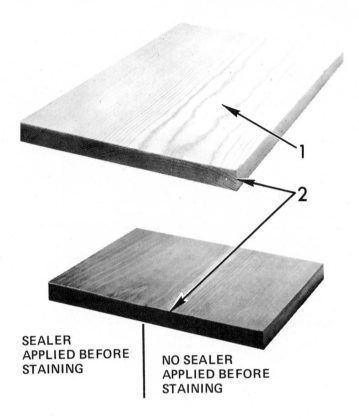

SEALER APPLIED BEFORE STAINING

NO SEALER APPLIED BEFORE STAINING

Applying Stains

The following tools and supplies are required to apply wood stain:

> Cloth. One clean, lint free cloth for application; one coarse, absorbent cloth for wiping.
> Turpentine or paint thinner, if required to remove stain
> Sealer, if desired
> Wood stain

There are minor differences in different brands of stain. Always read the manufacturer's instructions for specific details and recommended products such as types of thinner.

Wood stain should be stirred well before use and every 5 minutes during use to keep pigment from settling to bottom of container.

1. Using cloth saturated with stain, apply stain with long even strokes.

The longer the stain is left on the wood, the darker the surface will become.

2. Allow stain to penetrate surface for about 5 to 15 minutes or as determined from test.

Applying Stains

Wipe surface evenly to ensure uniform shade after staining.

The last stroke of wiping should be parallel with the wood grain. Wiping against the grain may leave streaks.

3.   Using absorbent cloth, wipe entire surface with long even strokes until surface appears dry.

If stain is wiped too soon or too briskly the color will be lightened. If darker color is desired, repeat Steps 1 through 3.

If stain is wiped too late, or has dried, the stain will be gummy and stick to the cloth. Go to Step 4.

If surface has desired color, go to Step 5 (below).

4.   Using cloth dampened with turpentine or thinner, clean surface of stain residue.

If surface now has desired color, go to Step 5 (below).

If surface is too light, repeat Steps 1 through 3.

Applying Stains

5.   Check surface for streak marks.

If surface has no streak marks, go to Step 7. Read information preceding Step 7.

If surface has streak marks, continue.

6.   Using cloth dampened with turpentine or thinner, rub marks until surface has uniform color.

If marks do not disappear, you may have to remove stain from entire surface and restain.

Before applying a finish coat, be sure to read manufacturer's instructions regarding resin sealers. Many stains include resin sealers in the stain. With this type stain, you can omit the process of sealer application. However, if a fine built-up finish is desired, a coat of sealer should always be applied.

7.   Using a brush, apply sealer to surface. Read Page 27 for applying sealer.

8.   Allow surface to dry as required before applying finish coat.

▶ **Description and Use**

Clear finishes are generally used on bare wood or stained wood surfaces to allow the natural color or grain to show. There are several different types of clear finishes, as described below.

● Varnishes — Varnishes have a resin base and resist scratching better than most other finishes. Spar varnishes are the most weather resistant of the clear finishes. The finish ranges from a satin to a gloss. When selecting a varnish, be sure it is compatible with the kind of use that you intend. Also determine the type of thinner that is recommended.

● Synthetics — These finishes are also called urethanes, polyurethanes, or plastic paints. Synthetics have the best combination of durability, long life, clarity, mar resistance, and short drying time of all finishes. As with varnish, synthetics range from a satin to a gloss finish and are soluble with recommended thinners. Synthetics must not be applied over shellac.

● Penetrating resins — These finishes soak into the wood to surround the wood fibers, providing a surface that resists abrasions, stains, and weather.

In addition to a tough surface, resin finishes also bring out the texture and beauty of natural wood. If the surface is scratched or damaged, simply apply more resin finish to blend the damaged area into the original surface.

● Shellacs — Shellac is a gum-based finish that mixes with shellac thinner only. It is easy to apply and repair. However, it is easily damaged by water. Water will leave white rings or spots on shellac surfaces.

● Lacquers — Lacquers are extremely flammable. They are soluble only with lacquer thinners. Because lacquer is fast drying, it is difficult for inexperienced persons to work with. The finish may be ruined if fresh lacquer is applied over partially dried lacquer. For best results, lacquer should be applied with an aerosol spray or spraying equipment.

▶ **Applying Varnishes and Synthetics**

This section can be used as a guide for applying synthetics and shellac. There are so many synthetic clear finishes on the market that the best procedure is to follow manufacturer's instructions on the label. Use this section on varnish application as a guide only.

Since wood grain will be seen through varnish, it is very important to correct any undesirable defects before varnishing.

When applying varnish to unfinished wood, be sure surface is free from dirt, wax and grease. If surface requires sanding, read section on sanding techniques, Page 18.

When applying varnish over stained wood, be sure surface has had sufficient drying time. If stained surface has dark spots, lighten these spots with extra fine grade finishing pads or No. 000 steel wool.

Always test varnish on a hidden part or a piece of identical wood. Keep in mind that varnish will darken the wood.

The following tools and supplies are required to apply varnish:

Tack rag [1]
Varnish brush [2]. Use 2-inch natural
    bristles with chiseled edge [3].
Artist's paintbrush, fine tip [4]
Metal container with wire stretched across
    opening [5]
Sandpaper, grade 400
Extra fine grade finishing pads or steel wool,
    No. 0000
Paint thinner, as recommended by
    manufacturer
Clean cloth

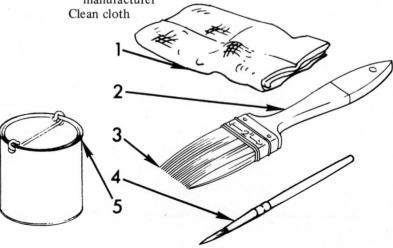

Applying Varnishes and Synthetics

Curved surfaces are a little more difficult to varnish than flat surfaces. When applying varnish to these surfaces always use a fairly dry brush. Be careful not to pull the brush over the edges of the turnings. This results in varnish sags or runs.

Corners and edges are also areas that require special care. If a brush stroke goes over an edge or outside corner, a sag will appear on a vertical surface.

All brush strokes should begin on the flat surface and go toward the edges. Upon reaching the edge, lift brush so that bristle tips just touch the edge before going off the surface.

On inside corners, brush strokes are just the opposite. Start in the corner and work toward the middle of the surface.

Always try to work on a horizontal surface. If possible, remove drawers, doors, etc. Place surface to be varnished in horizontal position.

Item to be varnished should be placed in lighted area and in an area that is as dust-free as possible. It should also be facing a window or light. This creates a reflection which will aid you in locating runs or dry spots.

CURVED SURFACE

THIS

NOT THIS

EDGE

OUTSIDE CORNER

INSIDE CORNER

Applying Varnishes and Synthetics

1. Place item in required position.

2. Dip varnish brush in thinner. Remove excess thinner from brush with cloth.

3. Stir varnish slowly and thoroughly. Allow varnish to stand until bubbles disappear.

If bubbles are present when varnish is applied, the bubbles will break as varnish dries causing small holes that are difficult to sand out.

4. Using tack rag, remove all sand dust from surface.

If surface to be varnished is large, such as a dining table, plan to work in smaller sections. Complete varnishing one section [1] before starting another section [2].

Work should be planned so that the start of a brush stroke is in an unvarnished area. It is difficult to begin a stroke in a wet area without leaving a brush mark.

5. Dip varnish brush into container about one third of bristle length. Remove excess varnish by pulling brush across strike wire [3].

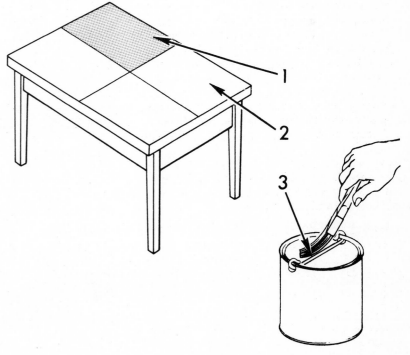

CLEAR FINISHES

Applying Varnishes and Synthetics

Varnish should be applied in bands. Coat should be thick and even.

Use no more than three or four back and forth strokes of brush. Varnish will not give a good finish if it is "scrubbed" on with too many back and forth strokes.

6. Brushing with the grain, apply three or more bands of varnish [1]. Space between bands is about the width of a brush.

7. Brushing across the grain, apply three or more bands of varnish [2].

8. Remove as much varnish as possible from brush by pulling brush across strike wire.

In next step, be sure to clean brush against strike wire after each stroke.

9. Brush lightly with the grain with only the tip of the brush touching the surface [3] to level any edges or runs.

10. Repeat Steps 6 through 9 until the surface is completely covered.

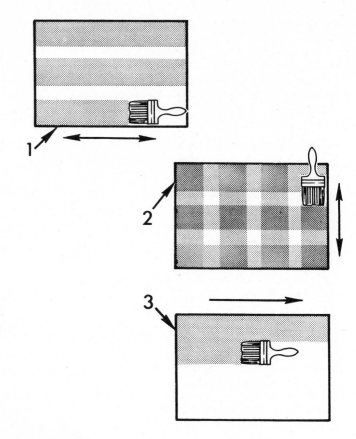

Applying Varnishes and Synthetics

If brush loses a bristle in the varnished surface, you can remove it by carefully jabbing at it with tip of brush [1] and picking it up. Smooth the varnish with a quick brush stroke.

If there is lint or dust lying on the top of the surface, the easiest way to remove it is as follows. Moisten the tip of an artist's brush and twist it into a fine point. Carefully touch point [2] to lint and lift straight up.

11. Check surface for any dry spots, runs or other blemishes.

If surface has blemishes and is still wet, go back to Step 9 (above).

If surface has blemishes and is damp or beginning to harden, leave blemishes until surface is dry. They will have to be sanded out and another coat applied.

If varnished surface is free of blemishes, continue to next page.

Applying Varnishes and Synthetics

Always read manufacturer's recommendations for drying time between coats. Generally allow at least 24 hours or, in damp weather, 36 hours for drying.

To provide a good surface for additional coats of varnish, surface should be sanded to remove gloss. Be sure not to sand through the finish, especially at the edges and high spots.

12.   Using sanding block and sandpaper, lightly sand surface until gloss and rough spots are removed.

Two coats of varnish will usually give a good clear finish. However, for a very fine, hard finish, apply three or four coats. Apply additional coats in same manner as first coat. Repeat Step 12 after each coat.

After the final coat has dried completely, surface may be lightly rubbed with steel wool to obtain a satin finish, or left as is to keep the glossy finish.

Sometimes a paste wax is recommended for initial polishing. For additional polishing, dust occasionally with a common household furniture polish.

▶ **Applying Penetrating Resins**

Penetrating resin finishes are among the most popular clear finishes in use today. They are easy to apply and they result in durable and beautiful finishes. They resist most household chemicals, water, alcohol, heat, and scratches. Because of these characteristics, they are suitable for finishing wood floors as well as furniture.

Penetrating resin soaks into the wood and the grain. It brings out the natural beauty of the wood itself with little or no change in wood color. It yields best results on open-grain wood such as oak, walnut, or teak. When used on close-grain woods, such as pine, the results are less spectacular.

Penetrating resin will slightly darken the natural color of wood such as oak or walnut. In these cases, it is probably not necessary to stain the wood.

If lighter finish is desired, a bleach should be applied to lighten the wood color first. Read Page 25.

If a darker color is desired, it may be necessary to apply a penetrating wiping stain. Read Page 31. The penetrating resin will not change the color of the stain, but will intensify it.

OAK

WITHOUT RESIN   WITH RESIN

WALNUT

WITHOUT RESIN   WITH RESIN

PINE

WITHOUT RESIN   WITH RESIN

39

Applying Penetrating Resins

If applying penetrating resin over a water stain or non-grain raising stain, expect a brighter color, some darkening and, possibly, red tones.

Always test the penetrating resin on a hidden area of the furniture or on a similar piece of wood.

The following tools and supplies are required to apply a penetrating resin finish:

> Clean cloth, lint free
> Extra fine grade finishing pads or steel wool, No. 000.
> Use to work resin into the wood.
> Paintbrush, if desired, to spread resin over surface

Always try to work on a horizontal surface. If possible, remove drawers, doors, etc. Place surface to be finished in horizontal position to aid the resin to penetrate the surface.

1. Place item so that surface to be finished is in horizontal position.

Applying Penetrating Resins

On curved or vertical surfaces, apply resin liberally with cloth. Inspect surface frequently for dull spots. Surface must be kept wet.

2. Pour a thick coat of penetrating resin onto flat surface [1].

3. Using finishing pad or steel wool [2], spread resin over surface with a slight pressure until surface is thickly coated.

Always read manufacturer's instructions for specific time allowed for resin to penetrate the wood. Also determine drying time required between coats. Some manufacturers recommend at least 1/2 to 1 hour for resin to penetrate the wood.

Dull spots on the surface indicate that all the resin has soaked into the wood. Additional resin should be applied in order to keep the surface wet for at least 1/2 hour while resin soaks into wood.

4. Apply additional resin as required.

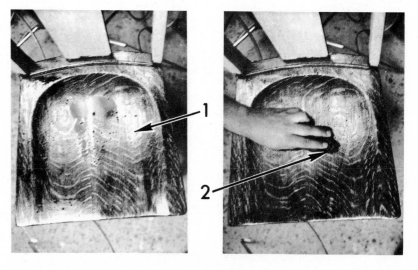

Applying Penetrating Resins

5. Using cloth, wipe surface clean of all resin. Do not leave any resin on surface.

6. Allow about three hours for resin to soak into wood before applying second coat.

A second coat should be applied. Resin finish will continue to soak into wood and fill the pores, even after surface has been wiped.

7. Repeat Steps 2 through 5 to apply additional resin.

8. Using a clean cloth, wipe surface dry.

9. Allow finish to dry thoroughly.

Paste wax has a tendency to clog the pores of the wood. This distracts from the natural beauty of the wood. Therefore, it is recommended that the beauty of the surface be preserved by occasional application of aerosol polish.

COLORED FINISHES

▶ **Description and Use**

Paint products are constantly changing and being improved. New paint materials are now longer lasting and easier to apply than before. For this reason always consult your paint dealer for the most recent information regarding paints.

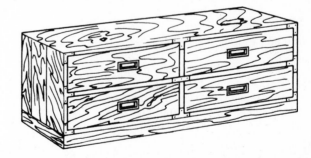

There are basically three reasons why a colored finish is used:

*   The wood does not have an attractive grain pattern.
*   The item may be constructed of several different kinds of wood; new and old, soft wood, hard wood, or possibly a mixture of all types. If a clear finish were applied, the result would be disappointing.
*   Often the surrounding area or room may need "cheering up". Using a colored finish on an item will add beauty as well as brighten the room.

COLORED FINISHES

Description and Use

Colored finishes are generally manufactured in the same manner as clear finishes. The most commonly used colored finish, enamel, is simply a varnish with color pigment added. Universal colorants or tints are also added to polyurethanes, lacquers, or shellacs to produce a colored finish.

Colored Shellac — Colored shellac is generally used as a primer and sealer to prevent wood knots and sap streaks from bleeding into finish coat. Always purchase shellac only in quantities needed for each job. Shellac will deteriorate if kept in storage. For additional information on shellac, see Page 36.

Colored Lacquer — Lacquer is made in three preparations: brush-on type, spray-on type, and aerosol cans.

The brush-on type is primarily made for use by professional refinishers. It is usually available through industrial supply stores. Brush-on lacquer is often used on hardwood floors.

The spray-on type, while more commonly available, requires application by spray equipment. To get professional-looking results requires considerable skill and experience in the use of this equipment.

Lacquer in aerosol cans is readily available in most paint stores, hardware stores, and builder's supply stores. The variety of colors is almost unlimited. The ready availability and ease of application of aerosol sprays make them especially suited for use by the home pro.

Lacquer contains very little color pigment. Therefore, several coats must be applied to properly cover an item. Because lacquer is extremely fast drying, many coats can be applied in one day. Go to Page 48 for applying aerosol finishes.

Description and Use

Enamels — A good-quality enamel is comparable to a good varnish, giving a fine finish and color. Enamel finishes range from flat to a gloss. Most enamels in use today can be divided into three separate groups:

- Alkyd base enamels — These enamels have an oil base and are soluble with paint thinner. They are durable and can be used either indoors or outdoors. Alkyd base enamels are self-leveling (brush marks disappear easily), resistant to rubbing, and easy to clean. For best results apply enamel with a brush, roller, or spray equipment.

- Urethane base enamels — This type of enamel is extremely durable and resists rubbing and chipping. They range from a satin finish to a gloss and are soluble with paint thinner. For best results they should be applied with either a brush or spray equipment.

- Acrylic base enamel — Acrylic base enamels, also called latex or vinyl enamels, are durable, easy to apply, and comparatively odorless. The big advantage is that they are water soluble. They are also self-leveling. Finish ranges from flat to semigloss. For best results apply with a brush, roller, or spray equipment.

▶ **Applying Undercoats**

Most paint manufacturers suggest using an undercoat or primer as the first coat. This undercoat is designed to provide a smooth, nonporous surface to which the topcoat can adhere. It fills the wood pores, similar to a sealer. For this reason a sealer is not necessary.

For best results, you should select the undercoat product which is recommended by the manufacturer of the topcoat (finish) which you plan to use. This will ensure that the undercoat and finish are compatible.

Undercoat is usually white and may show through the topcoats. For this reason it is recommended that the undercoat be tinted by adding a little of the topcoat color to it.

One of the best undercoats to use on metal is zinc chromate primer. This primer is designed to inhibit rust on metal surfaces as well as act as an undercoat for enamels. It may be purchased either in an aerosol spray or in liquid form.

There are also paints with rust inhibitors already added. It may not be necessary to use metal primers with these paints. In all cases, however, be sure that the surface is completely free of rust and corrosion before applying primers or paint.

Applying Undercoats

The following tools and supplies are required to apply an undercoat:

    Paintbrush [1]. Use two-inch natural bristle brush with a chiseled edge [2]. Undercoat. Use undercoat recommended by manufacturer of finish.

1. Stir paint thoroughly. Do not shake container. Shaking container will cause bubbles in undercoat which may be difficult to cover with topcoat.

When dipping the brush into paint, do not submerge bristles more than halfway [3].

The first time brush is dipped into undercoat, gently stir undercoat with the brush to separate the bristles.

2. Dip brush into undercoat. Lift brush straight up to prevent separation of bristles [4]. If bristles separate, brush will leave brush marks on surface.

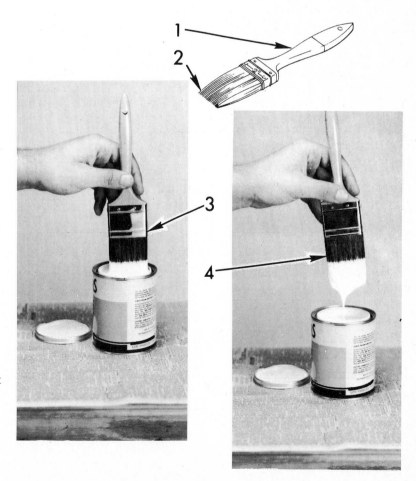

COLORED FINISHES

Applying Undercoats

Always work under sufficient lighting. Lighting should be at an angle so that the reflection will aid you in locating dry spots and runs.

The undercoat should be applied to a small area at a time to ensure an even, smooth coat. Be careful to avoid splattering of the paint. This will cause raised spots on the surface which will be difficult to conceal.

3. Apply undercoat evenly and smoothly, brushing across the grain [1].

If undercoat runs, brush it out with an almost dry brush.

4. Brush lightly with the grain [2] until undercoat appears even and smooth.

If brush loses a bristle in the painted surface, you can remove it by carefully jabbing at it with tip of brush and picking it up. Smooth area with a light brush stroke, lifting the brush near the end of the stroke.

5. Repeat Steps 3 and 4 until undercoat covers entire surface.

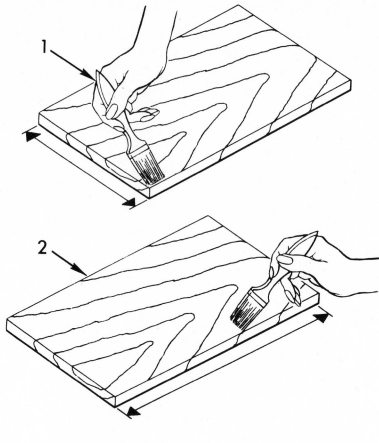

▶ Applying Colored Finishes

The following tools and supplies are required to apply a colored finish:

> Paintbrush [1]. Use two-inch natural bristle brush with a chiseled edge [2].
> Tack rag [3]
> Artist's paintbrush [4]. Use fine-tipped brush.
> Metal container with wire stretched across opening [5].
> Sandpaper, fine
> Extra fine grade finishing pads or steel wool, No. 0000
> Paint thinner

Curved surfaces are a little more difficult to paint than flat surfaces. When applying paint to these surfaces, always use a fairly dry brush. Be careful not to pull the brush over the edges of the turnings. This results in sags or runs.

Corners and edges also require special care. If a brush stroke goes over an edge or outside corner, a sag will appear on a vertical surface.

All brush strokes should begin on the flat surface and go toward the edges. Upon reaching the edge, lift brush so that tip of bristles just touch the edge before going off the surface.

On inside corners, brush strokes are just the opposite. Start in the corner and work toward the middle of the surface.

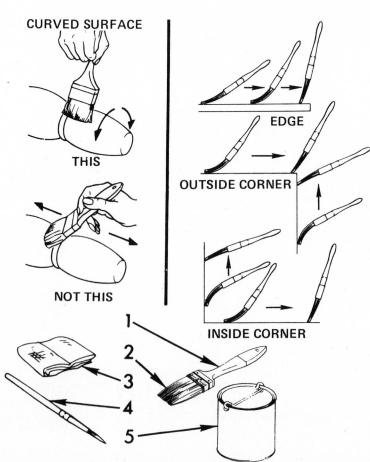

CURVED SURFACE

THIS

NOT THIS

EDGE

OUTSIDE CORNER

INSIDE CORNER

Applying Colored Finishes

Always try to work on a horizontal surface. If possible, remove drawers, doors, etc. Place surface to be painted in horizontal position.

Item to be painted should be placed in a well-lighted area. Area should be as dust free as possible. Item should be facing a window or light. This creates a reflection which will aid you in locating runs or dry spots.

1. Place item in required position.

2. Dip brush in thinner. Remove excess thinner from brush with cloth.

3. Stir paint slowly and thoroughly. Allow paint to stand until any bubbles disappear.

If bubbles are present when paint is applied, the bubbles will break as paint dries, causing small holes that are difficult to sand out.

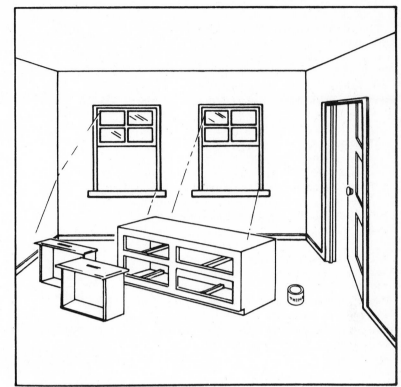

Applying Colored Finishes

4. Using tack rag, remove all dust from surface.

If surface to be painted is large, such as a table, plan to work in smaller sections. Complete painting one section [1] before starting another section [2].

Work should be planned so that the start of a brush stroke is in an unpainted area. It is difficult to begin a stroke in a wet area without leaving a brush mark.

5. Dip brush into container about one third of bristle length. Remove excess paint by pulling brush across strike wire [3].

Paint should be applied in bands. Coat should be thick and even.

Use no more than three or four back and forth strokes of brush. Paint will not give a good finish if it is "scrubbed" on with too many back and forth strokes.

6. Brushing with the grain, apply three or more bands of paint [4]. Space between bands is about the width of a brush.

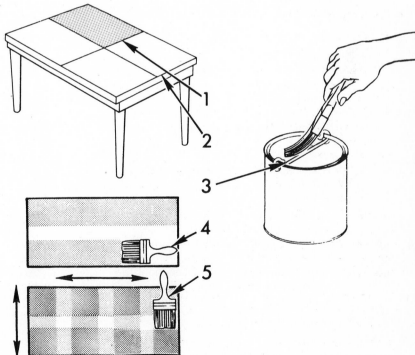

7. Brushing across the grain, apply three or four more bands of paint [5].

8. Remove as much paint as possible from brush by pulling brush across strike wire [3].

COLORED FINISHES

Applying Colored Finishes

In next step, be sure to clean brush against strike wire after each stroke.

9. Brush lightly with the grain with only the tips of the brush touching the surface [1] to level any edges or runs.

10. Repeat Steps 6 through 9 until the surface is completely covered.

If brush loses a bristle in the painted surface, you can remove it by carefully jabbing at it with tip of brush [2] and picking it up. Smooth the paint with a quick brush stroke.

If there is lint or dust lying on the top of the surface, the easiest way to remove it is as follows. Moisten the tip of an artist's brush and twist it into a fine point. Carefully touch point [3] to lint and lift straight up.

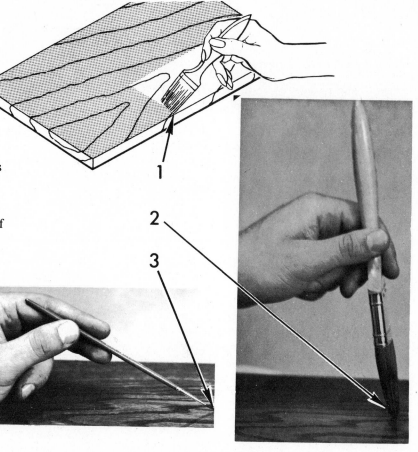

Applying Colored Finishes

11. Check surface for any dry spots, runs or other blemishes.

If surface has blemishes and is still wet, go back to Step 9 (above).

If surface has blemishes and is damp or beginning to harden, leave blemishes until surface is dry. They will have to be sanded out and another coat applied.

If painted surface is free of blemishes, continue.

Always read manufacturer's recommendations for drying time between coats. Generally, allow at least 24 hours or, in damp weather, 36 hours for drying.

To provide a good surface for additional coats of paint, surface should be sanded to remove the gloss. Be sure not to sand through the finish, especially at the edges and high spots.

12. Using sanding block and sandpaper, lightly sand surface until gloss and rough spots are removed.

Two coats of paint will usually give a good clear finish. However, for a very fine, hard finish, apply three or four coats. Apply additional coats in same manner as first coat.

After the final coat has dried completely, surface may be lightly rubbed with steel wool to obtain a satin finish, or left as is to keep the glossy finish.

After the final coat has dried completely, surface may be lightly rubbed with finishing pad or steel wool to obtain a satin finish, or left as is to keep the glossy finish.

Sometimes a paste wax is recommended for initial polishing. For additional polishing, dust occasionally with a common household furniture polish.

▶ **Description and Use**

The variety of aerosol paint products is continually expanding. Almost any finish and color is now available in aerosol spray preparations.

Aerosol spray paints are generally much more expensive than brush-on paints. For that reason, they may not be very practical for finishing large surfaces. However, they are easy to use and, when properly applied, can give excellent results. They are the home pro's answer to many otherwise tedious painting jobs such as patio furniture, chairs, shutters, and bicycles. On items such as these, the finish can be not only better looking but also much faster to apply than brush-on paints.

The biggest problem in using spray paints is the overspray or mist. The spray is extremely difficult to confine to the immediate work area. Small particles will drift and settle on surrounding areas.

It is important that you take time to screen the work area and protect all nearby items. Otherwise, cleanup will be a time-consuming, difficult job. If at all possible, do your spraying outdoors or in a garage rather than in the house.

If you can spray outdoors, do it on a calm day or in an area completely protected from the wind.

If you must spray indoors, do it in a well-ventilated area. Open windows and doors. If you have a fan, it is a good idea to exhaust the fumes to the outside.

WARNING

Aerosol paints are flammable. Be sure that there are no open flames such as pilots for gas clothes dryers or water heaters in the work area.

Description and Use

An adequate screen or spray booth can be constructed using common household items in the following manner:

1. Stretch a clothes line [1] across the work area.

2. Hang an old sheet or shower curtain over the clothes line.

3. Place old sheets [2] or plastic drop cloths over the floor area and nearby items to protect them from the overspray.

Although using a spray can is quite easy, it is suggested that you practice using the techniques as described in this section before applying the finish to your work surface.

Always move the can in a straight uniform manner [3]. The painting stroke should be made by moving the can at a right angle and parallel to the surface. If the can is moved in an arc [4] instead of parallel to the surface, the resulting finish will be poorly distributed. Too heavy a coat will be applied in the center and a very thin coat at the ends of the stroke.

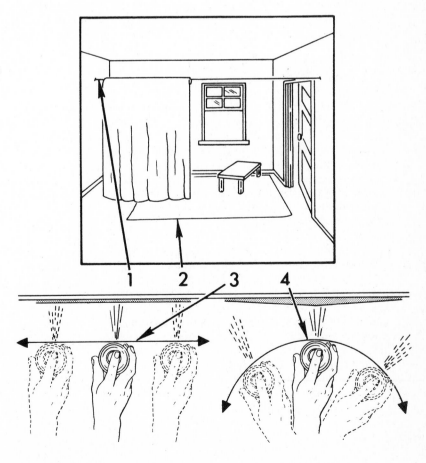

▶ Applying Aerosol Finishes

You should practice a few strokes on old cartons or newspapers before applying the finish to the actual surface. This allows you to determine the pattern of the spray. Most aerosol spray patterns are either fan shaped [1] or cone shaped [2].

When spraying a flat surface, first apply a single vertical stroke [3] at each end. This will help reduce overspraying and will ensure more complete coverage.

Always try to complete a full stroke. If you move unevenly or stop in mid-stroke, you will cause runs, sags, or buildup of excess paint. The speed of each stroke should be about the same as you would use with a brush.

Be sure that each stroke overlaps [4] the preceding stroke by one-half. This will ensure a full, wet coat without streaks.

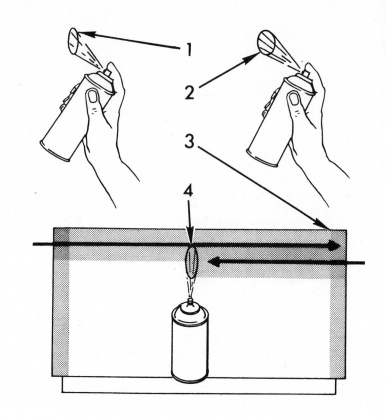

Applying Aerosol Finishes

The distance from the spray nozzle to the work surface should be about 12 to 15 inches. If the nozzle is held closer to the surface, too much paint will be applied, causing runs and sags [1]. If the nozzle is held farther away from the surface, particles of paint will begin to dry before reaching the surface. The resulting finish [2] will be gritty and rough.

Be sure to read manufacturer's instructions before applying the finish. Often these products differ in their requirements for surface preparation and application.

After each use, be sure to turn the can [3] upside down and press the tip until spray from nozzle is free of paint. After clearing the nozzle, always wipe it clean to prevent clogging.

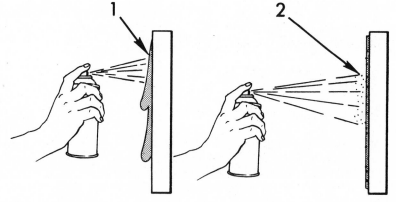

Applying Aerosol Finishes

In addition to the general techniques previously
described, there are some specific spraying techniques that you should know. They are described
as follows:

- Flat Surfaces, next section (below).
- Inside Corners, Page 50.
- Outside Corners, Page 50.
- Cylindrical Shapes and Small Round Objects,
  Page 50.

▶ **Applying Aerosol Finishes to Flat Surfaces**

When spraying a flat, vertical surface, perform
Steps 1 and 2.

1. Apply a single vertical stroke [1] at each
   end of surface.

2. Apply horizontal strokes [2] to surface until
   covered. Be sure that each stroke overlaps
   the preceding stroke by one-half.

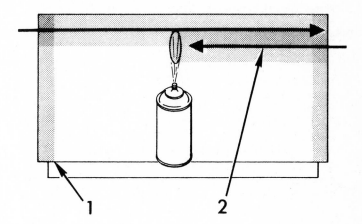

Applying Aerosol Finishes to Flat Surfaces

When spraying a flat level surface, perform
Steps 3 and 4.

3. Spray edges [1] of surface first.

4. Apply horizontal strokes [2] to the surface.
   Begin at the edge nearest you and work
   toward the far edge. This helps prevent
   overspray on the painted surface.

When spraying a long narrow panel, perform
Steps 5 and 6.

5. Apply a horizontal stroke [3] at each of the
   longer edges.

6. Apply vertical strokes [4] to remaining
   surface. Be sure that each stroke overlaps
   the preceding stroke by one-half.

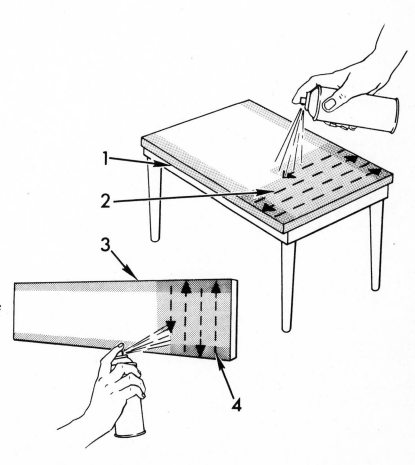

AEROSOL FINISHES

▶ **Applying Aerosol Finishes to Inside Corners**

Either of the two methods, Step 7 or Step 8, may be used to spray inside corners.

7. Apply spray directly into corner [1]. This method is fast and practical. However, the coating will not be as uniform as the method in Step 8.

8. Apply spray to one side [2]. Then apply spray to other side [3].

▶ **Applying Aerosol Finishes to Outside Corners**

9. Apply a vertical stroke down the tip [4] of the corner. Position the can so that the edge of the corner divides the spray pattern in half.

▶ **Applying Aerosol Finishes to Cylindrical Shapes and Small Round Objects**

10. Place item on one end. Apply spray to surface either crosswise [5] or vertically [6]. Overlap each preceding stroke.

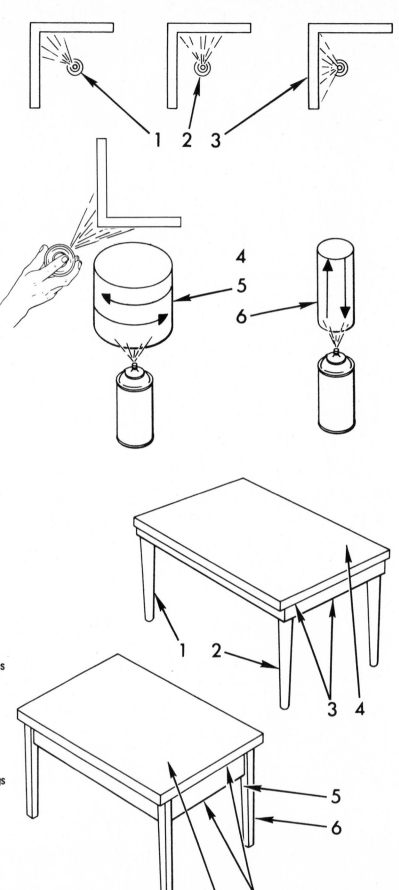

These instructions describe the sequence of spraying the following items:

Tables, next section (below).

Chest and Drawers, Page 51.

Chairs, Page 51.

All surfaces which are not to be painted must be thoroughly protected from spray mist and over-spray. Use newspapers and masking tape to cover these surfaces.

▶ **Applying Aerosol Finishes to Table with Round Legs**

Spray in the following sequence:

Inside surface [1] of each leg
Outside surface [2] of each leg
All edges [3]
Top [4]

▶ **Applying Aerosol Finishes to Table with Square Legs**

2. Spray in the following sequence:

Two inside surfaces [5] of each leg
Working on one side of table at a time,
    Outside surface [6] of legs
    Edges [7]
Top [8]

50

▶ **Applying Aerosol Finishes to Chest and Drawers**

1. Remove drawers [1] or doors.

2. Remove or cover handles of drawers and other surfaces or hardware not to be painted.

3. Spray surfaces in the following sequence:

   Drawers [1] or doors
   Inside chest [2], if desired
   Back [3], if desired
   One side [4]
   Front [5]
   Other side [6]
   Top [7]

4. Remove cover from protected surfaces.

5. Allow to dry completely.

6. Install handles and other hardware. Install door or insert drawers.

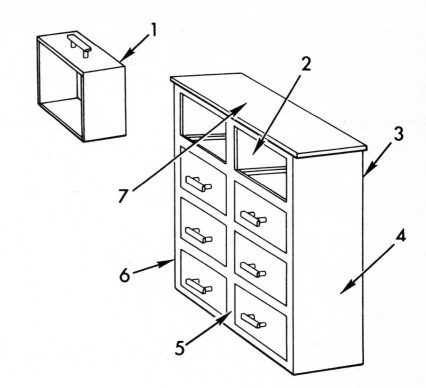

▶ **Applying Aerosol Finishes to Chairs**

1. Turn chair upside down resting on edge of seat and back.

2. Spray legs [1] and rungs [2].

3. Place chair right side up.

4. Spray back [3] and side posts [4].
   Spray back and front of panel [5].

5. Spray edges [6] of seat.

6. Spray seat [7]. Allow to dry completely.

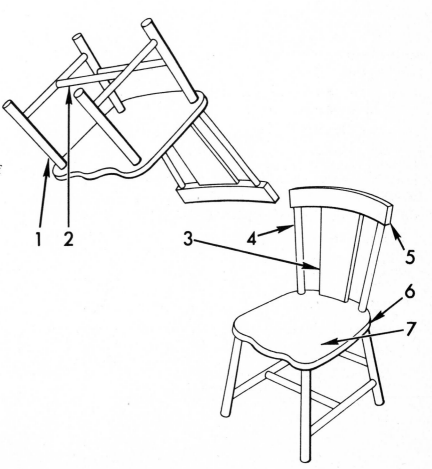

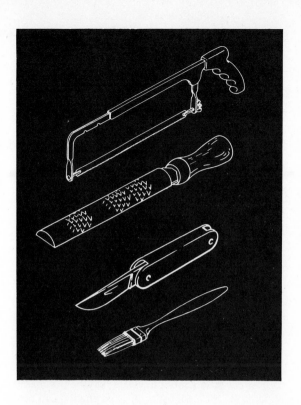

ANTIQUING

Antiquing is a painting process that is used to simulate an antique or aged appearance. It is one of the simplest and most popular methods of refinishing old furniture. One of the advantages is that this method eliminates or reduces the need for preparation such as stripping off the old finish, sanding, and filling.

Many complete antiquing kits are available which include all materials required for antiquing. Generally, these kits contain a base coat, an antiquing glaze, sandpaper, paintbrush, lint-free wiping cloth, and a sponge or similar grain-making tool.

Most kits are designed so that you may complete the antiquing process in one day. The paints in this type of kit are water-base latex paints. These paints dry rapidly and tools can be easily cleaned with water.

If desired, base coats and glazes may be purchased separately. Since most semi-gloss enamel can be used as the base coat, it is easy to make up your own color scheme. Most glazes are available only in dark brown or black.

Some original antiquing effects may be produced by applying a dark glaze over a bright-colored base coat such as a green, blue, orange, or other color.

Prior to antiquing, go to the next section (below) for information on surface preparation and procedures to follow when determining if the old finish should be removed.

■■■ PREPARING THE SURFACE ■■■

This section describes the procedures that should be followed to properly prepare an old or unfinished surface prior to antiquing. The basic purpose is to help you obtain a sound, clean surface that is necessary for a durable and beautiful antique finish.

You will save a great deal of time and work if you do not have to remove the old finish. Therefore, determining if it is necessary to remove the old finish is important. The procedures described in Checking the Surface, Page 55, will aid you in determining the soundness of the old finish.

Even if the old finish is sound, there is a chance that the old finish is dirty or has several layers of old wax. This will prevent proper bonding of the new finish to the old surface. The procedures in Cleaning the Old Finish, Page 55, describe some common methods used to clean dirt and wax from an old finish.

An antique finish may be applied to a wood, metal, or plaster surface. The Minor Repair section contains procedures for removing defects in these surfaces.

Repairs in wood surfaces have been described in the Refinishing section. Refer to Preparing the Surface, Page 2.

For metal repairs, the procedures describe removal of dents and several methods of treating rust and corrosion.

For plaster repairs, the procedures describe replacement of broken or missing molded pieces and repair of hairline cracks.

The sanding techniques and methods necessary to properly prepare a surface for an antique finish are the same as previously described in the Refinishing section, Page 18.

▶ **Checking the Surface**

An antique finish can be applied over an existing finish only if the old finish is in good condition. Any flaking, peeling, or cracking requires the old finish to be removed. Go to Page 3 to remove the old finish if required. Then continue.

The surface of the item, whether bare wood or old finish, must be smooth and even with no chipped edges or corners. If the surface is rough, uneven, or chipped, it must be sanded smooth. Go to Page 18 for sanding techniques.

If the old finish is not removed, it must be thoroughly cleaned before antiquing. Go to next section (below) to clean the old finish.

If the old finish is removed, an undercoat or primer is required before antiquing. Page 43 describes application of an undercoat or primer. After application, go to Page 61 to begin antiquing.

▶ **Cleaning the Old Finish**

In most cases the old finish is too dirty or too glossy to accept a new finish without peeling off due to poor adhesion. Over a period of time, even with proper care, layers of dirt, wax, and grease tend to build up on the surface.

There are two common cleaners used to remove the dirt and wax: detergent and water, and tri-sodium phosphate (T.S.P.) and water. The two common deglossers described in this section are commercial deglossers and sandpaper.

▶ **Cleaning the Old Finish with Detergent and Water**

1. Using a solution of warm water and detergent, clean surface thoroughly with a scrub brush.

2. Rinse surface with water. Allow surface to dry thoroughly.

3. Apply a commercial deglosser or sandpaper to remove gloss from painted surface. Page 56.

▶ **Cleaning the Old Finish with
Trisodium Phosphate (T.S.P.) and Water**

1. Following manufacturer's recommended measurements, mix T.S.P. with water.

2. Thoroughly wash surface. Rinse well with water. Allow to dry thoroughly.

3. Apply a commercial deglosser or sandpaper to remove gloss from painted surface. See text below.

Using Commercial Deglossers

Commercial deglossers act as "sandpaper" in a liquid form, dissolving wax and grease while removing the shine or gloss at the same time.

WARNING

Be sure to read cautions or warnings on label of liquid deglossers.

Carefully follow manufacturer's instructions on label for best results to remove wax, grease and gloss from surface.

Using Sandpaper

Sandpaper is ideally suited for small items. Go to Page 18 for information on sandpapers and sanding techniques.

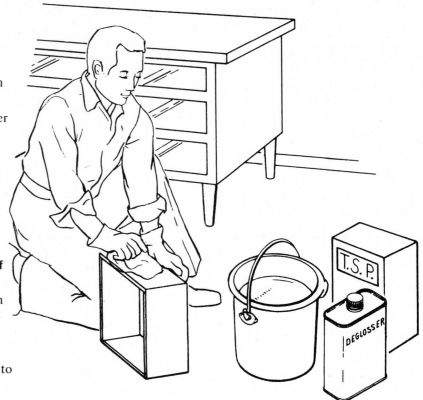

▶ **Minor Metal Repairs**

The procedures on this page apply only to slight, accessible dents in thin metal. To repair large dents or dents in thick metal, go to Page 57.

First try to push the dent out with your hand. If this method does not work, an easy method is described below.

The following tools and supplies are required to remove a small dent:

> Wooden or rawhide mallet [1], used instead of steel hammer to minimize surface damage.
> Sandbag [2], which can be made by filling thick plastic bag or cloth sack with sand.

1. Place dented surface [3] snugly against sandbag [2].

CAUTION

Use mallet carefully to prevent further damage to surface. Do not hammer out dent beyond surrounding surface.

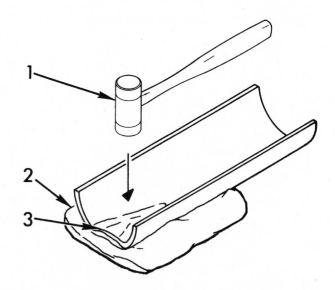

2. Using mallet, carefully tap out dent [3] even with surrounding surface.

3. Go to Page 58 to prepare the entire surface for antiquing.

Minor Metal Repairs

To repair large dents or dents in thick metal, the dented surface must be filled with a commercial automobile body putty.

The following tools and supplies are required to repair dents in metal:

> Power drill [1]
> Drill bit [2], 1/4-inch or smaller
> Putty knife [3]
> Automobile body putty
> Sandpaper, several grit sizes ranging from
>   50 (coarse) to 180 (fine)

1. Using drill and bit, make several small holes in dented area [4].

2. Using coarsest sandpaper, sand dented area thoroughly.

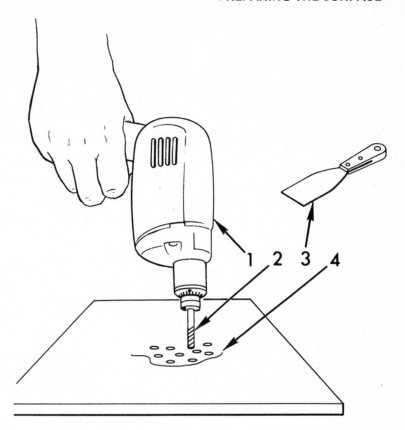

Minor Metal Repairs

Be sure to follow manufacturer's instructions on label of automobile body putty for mixing procedures and drying times. Some brands of putty are a ready to use paste and require no mixing.

3. Mix putty, if required.

In next step, putty must be applied with enough pressure to completely fill the drilled holes to ensure proper bonding of putty to metal.

4. Using putty knife, fill dented area [1] until putty is slightly higher than surrounding area.

5. Allow putty to dry thoroughly.

6. Using sandpaper in decreasing coarseness, sand area [2] until level with surrounding area.

7. Go to Page 58 to prepare the entire surface for antiquing.

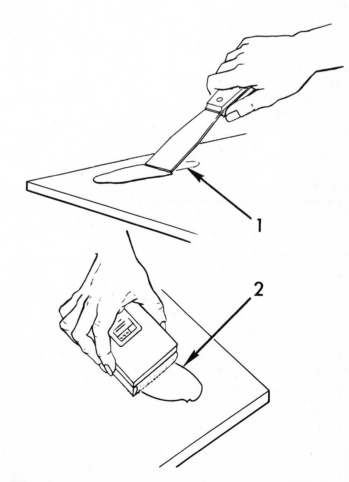

Minor Metal Repairs

Before applying any finish, the surface must be free of all traces of rust and corrosion. Rust or corrosion will appear on any unprotected metal surface. Some of the methods used to remove rust or corrosion are described below.

- Wire brush attachments [1] for power drills [2]. These are available in coarse and fine grades. The attachments are best suited for removal of rust from larger areas.

- Wire brushes [3]. Wire brushes are excellent for removing rust from small areas and curved areas. They also serve as general-purpose cleaning tools for most metal items found in the home.

- Steel wool. Steel wool is used for removing rust from corners, small intricate areas and aluminum surfaces. It is made in several grades from very coarse to very fine.

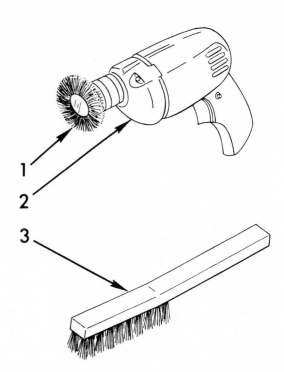

Minor Metal Repairs

- Emery cloth [1]. Emery cloth is ideal for smaller projects and for metal polishing. As with steel wool, it is made in varying grades of coarse to fine grits.

- Commercial rust remover [2]. There are many types of chemical products used to remove rust and corrosion. They are available in liquid, paste or jelly form. The jellied type is easy to apply, removes rust well, and rinses off with water. When buying a rust remover for aluminum work, be sure the manufacturer recommends his product for aluminum corrosion.

After all traces of rust or corrosion have been removed, the surface should be coated either with a metal primer, such as zinc chromate primer, or with a rust-inhibitor paint. It is recommended that the primer coat be lightly sanded (using about grade 150 sandpaper) to remove wire brush or steel wool marks. If not sanded, these marks may show through the final finish.

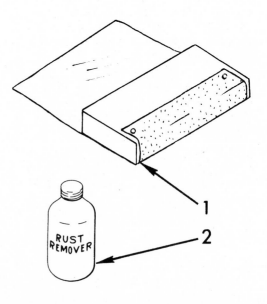

58

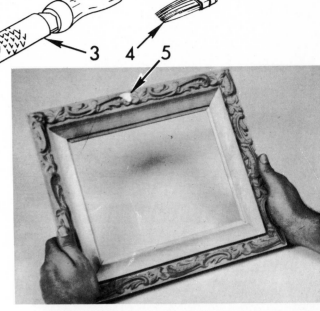

▶ Minor Plaster Repairs

Many raised patterns on picture frames, tables, etc., are actually molded plaster, not carved wood as they appear. If a piece of the pattern [5] is broken, the following procedure describes a method of replacing the broken plaster. If the plaster is just cracked or scratched, go to Page 61 for its repair.

The following tools and supplies are required to replace broken plaster patterns:

    Hacksaw [1] or hacksaw blade only
    Knife [2]
    File [3]
    1/2-inch artist's brush [4]
    Plaster of paris or powdered spackling
       compound
    Modeling clay
    White glue
    Sandpaper, 220 Grade extra fine

Minor Plaster Repairs

The damaged plaster [1] must be shaped to allow a new piece to be installed in its place. The loose plaster can be scraped off, or the damage can be completely removed.

The best method is to cut out the damaged piece [3] completely. Make cuts [5] square and even. Provide a flat surface [4] for joining the new piece.

1.   Carefully remove damaged plaster [3].

2.   Locate a pattern [2] that is identical to the damaged piece [3].

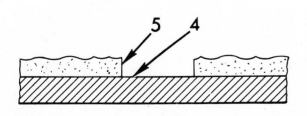

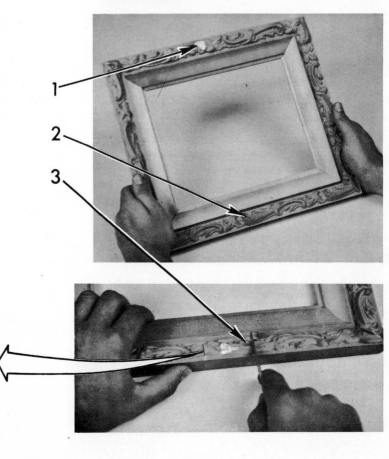

PREPARING THE SURFACE

Minor Plaster Repairs

3. Using modeling clay [1], make an impression of the area identical to the damaged area. Be sure to press clay firmly over entire surface for good impression.

4. Carefully remove modeling clay from pattern. Check that full impression [2] has been made. The clay may have to be reapplied.

5. Mix the plaster of paris as recommended by manufacturer's instructions.

6. Fill impression [2] with plaster of paris. Allow plaster to dry thoroughly.

7. Remove clay from around new plaster pattern.

New molded pattern [3] may require trimming to fit properly in damaged area [4].

8. Using knife or file, carefully trim new plaster pattern [3] as required.

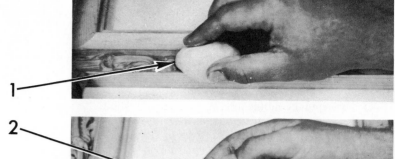

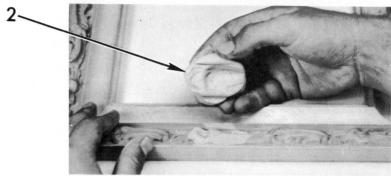

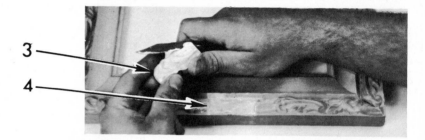

Minor Plaster Repairs

9. Apply glue to back of new plaster pattern [1] and to damaged surface [2].

10. Press new pattern [1] into place. Allow glue to dry thoroughly.

11. Mix another batch of plaster. Make plaster thin enough so it can be brushed on.

12. Using brush and plaster, fill all gaps [3] and seams between new pattern and surface. Allow plaster to dry thoroughly.

13. Using sandpaper, smooth any rough or uneven spots on new pattern [4].

It is recommended that a primer or undercoat be applied to the unfinished area before finishing.

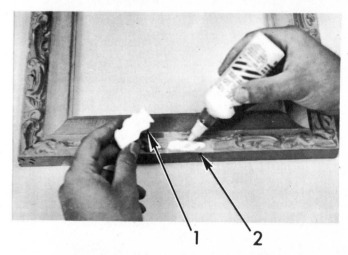

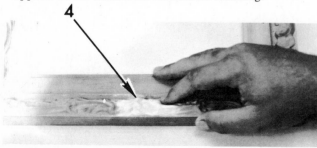

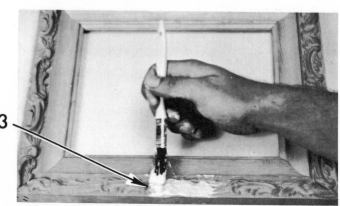

Minor Plaster Repairs

Hairline cracks [3] are very fine, small cracks that appear on molded patterns [2]. These procedures describe repair of cracks and deep scratches.

The following tools and supplies are required to repair cracks and scratches in molded plaster:

> Camel-hair brush [1], fine tip
> Powdered spackling compound
> Clean, lint-free cloth

1. Mix a very thin paste of spackling compound according to manufacturer's instructions.

It may require several applications of spackling compound to properly fill the cracks [3] and scratches.

Always work carefully and take your time when applying compound to avoid getting spackle on surrounding pattern [2].

2. Using brush, apply spackling compound to cracks [3] and scratches.

3. Dampen cloth. Wipe excess spackle from surrounding area with cloth.

4. Allow spackle to dry thoroughly.

5. Repeat Steps 2 through 4 until all cracks [3] and scratches have been completely filled.

Surface is now ready for finishing.

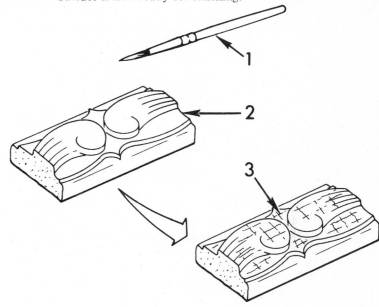

ANTIQUING

The antiquing process is quite easy. Before you begin, you may want the surface to show dents, scratches, etc., to emphasize the aged look. These effects should be applied before applying the base coat. See section on Decorating Effects, Page 65.

After achieving desired surface effects, a base coat is applied to cover existing grain and finish. After base coat, the glaze is applied and wiped away. The result is an aged appearance suggesting normal wear, rather than just a painted surface. For a more beautiful and longer lasting finish, most manufacturers recommend a semigloss coat of clear finish be applied to the finished surface.

Although in this section the antiquing process is described by application on furniture, it may also be applied to metal or plaster.

Van Meer

▶ Applying Base Coat

The following tools and supplies are required to apply the base coat:

> Nylon bristle paintbrush [1]. Width should be as wide as possible for surface being painted
> Sanding block [2]
> Sandpaper, fine grade
> Newspapers or drop cloth
> Base coat paint

Before application of base coat, be sure the following tasks have been accomplished:

- All handles, knobs and other hardware are removed

- Surface is free of dirt and wax

- All drawers and doors are removed

- Mirrors have been protected by paper and tape

- Glossy surfaces have been lightly sanded with 150 grade sandpaper or No. 000 steel wool

Select a warm, well ventilated work area to aid in drying.

On some old furniture, an undercoat or primer should be applied before the base coat to prevent the old finish from bleeding through. Page 43.

On unfinished or very dark finished surfaces, two base coats or an undercoat or primer should be applied. Page 43.

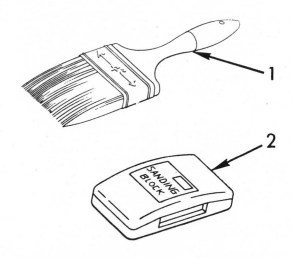

Applying Base Coat

1. Place item on newspapers or drop cloth.

Plan work so that the start of a brush stroke is in an unpainted area. If started in a wet area, it often leaves brush marks.

2. Stir base coat thoroughly. Dip brush into base coat about one-half bristle length.

Do not pull bristles across edge of container. This may cause bristles to separate and leave brush marks on finish.

3. Gently tap bristles against inside of container to remove excess paint.

4. Apply a thick base coat over a small area, brushing evenly and smoothly with the grain.

Applying Base Coat

Be sure final brush strokes are with the direction of the grain.

Do not try to touch up areas that appear dull or flat. Base coats dry quickly, so will appear dull in spots.

5.   Apply base coat in even strokes until entire surface is covered.

6.   With only tips of bristles [1] touching surface, lightly brush with the grain to any edges or runs.

7.   Allow surface to dry according to manufacturer's recommendations.

8.   Check surface for complete coverage. Apply additional base coat where needed.

9.   Using sanding block [2] and sandpaper, lightly sand entire surface.

If more than one base coat is desired, repeat Steps 5 through 9.

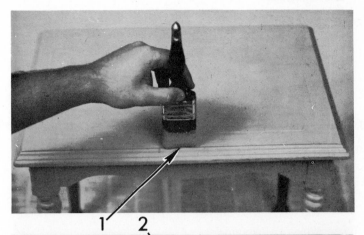

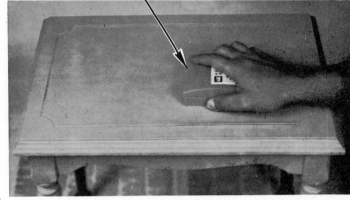

▶ Applying Antique Glaze

The following tools and supplies are required to apply antique glaze:

> Paintbrush [1]
> Clean, lint-free cloth
> Antique glaze

Be sure base coat is thoroughly dry before applying glaze.

1.   Stir glaze thoroughly.

2.   Dip brush into glaze about one-half bristle length.

Always work on one surface at a time. Apply glaze and wipe this surface until desired antique effect is obtained. Then go to next surface.

3.   Apply a thin coat of glaze to selected surface.

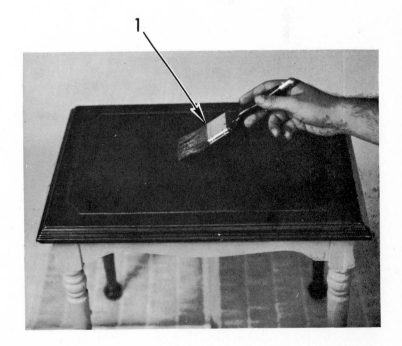

ANTIQUING

Applying Antique Glaze

Always read manufacturer's recommendations for specific drying time. Some brands do not require a "setting" time before wiping.

The more glaze that is wiped off, the lighter the final tone. The less wiped off, the darker the final tone will be. For best "antique" results, methods described should be followed when wiping glaze.

- Wipe the hardest on edges, corners, etc., of top surfaces to simulate normal wear.

- Wipe carvings, grooves, or scratches very lightly to enhance antique appearance of these areas.

- On large flat surfaces, try to blend glaze from light in center to darker shades toward the edges. At the edges, wipe glaze thinner.

- Always remove a little glaze at a time. It is easier to wipe again than to apply an additional coat.

4. Using clean, lint-free cloth, remove glaze as desired.

Applying Antique Glaze

After desired amount of glaze has been removed, allow item to remain overnight to ensure sufficient drying time.

Check surface again for desired effects. If more glaze needs removal, use extra fine grade finishing pads, No. 000 steel wool [1], or 220 grade extra fine sandpaper. If too much glaze has been removed, an additional coat will have to be applied.

After desired effects has been obtained, some manufacturers recommend either waxing or applying a semigloss varnish to the surface. This results in a more durable surface.

If waxing, apply manufacturer's recommended wax. Then go to Step 7. If applying varnish, continue.

5. Apply a semigloss varnish. See Page 36 for instructions.

6. Allow surface to dry thoroughly.

7. Install all doors and drawers. Install all hardware.

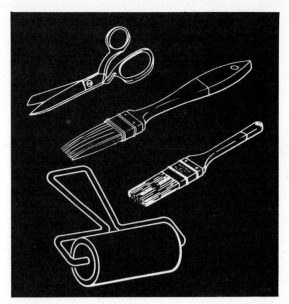

DECORATING EFFECTS

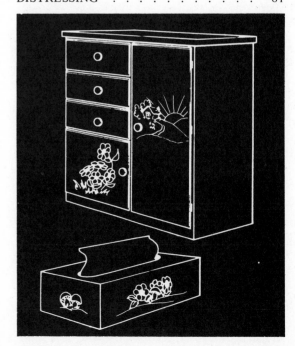

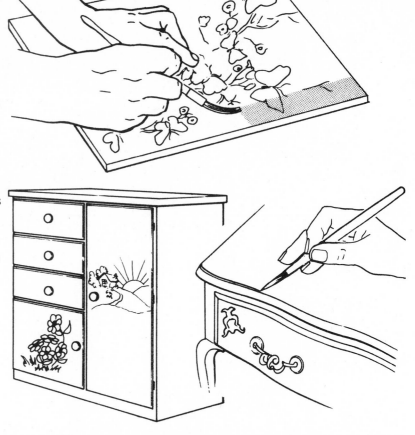

The special effects described in this section add to the beauty of the final finish. Some of the procedures are mainly for decoration, while others are applied to simulate a worn and aged appearance.

It is suggested that you read through the entire section before deciding upon a particular technique. This may give you additional ideas. If this is the case, you should still follow the appropriate procedures as a guide.

If you are trying to simulate a particular furniture style or period of time, you should try to find a picture of an identical item. This will enable you to duplicate it as closely as possible.

■■ **HIGHLIGHTING** ■■■■■■

Highlighting is a decorating technique generally applied to parts of flat surfaces, raised areas of carvings, and on turnings. Highlighting is also known as shading or blending.

The purpose of highlighting is to simulate the effects of normal wear and years of exposure and waxing. Highlighting is usually accomplished when you antique an item. Page 54.

To obtain the appearance of age on a flat surface, lighten the center area and leave the edges dark. This is done by wiping the glaze before it dries. On raised areas of carvings, wipe the glaze from the high spots, but leave the glaze in the lower areas and crevices. This gives the effect of repeated waxing and rubbing.

If the glaze has already dried, highlights may be obtained by carefully sanding the surfaces lightly. Use extra fine grade finishing pads, very fine sandpaper (220 grade or finer), or fine steel wool (000 grade) before applying the clear finish.

Graining is a decorating technique used to create a natural wood grain appearance on a painted surface. The appearance of the simulated grain is dependent upon the type of graining tool used.

Many common items found around the home may be used to produce a natural-looking wood grain. For example, a sponge, piece of cheesecloth, dry stiff-bristle brush, or scrap piece of carpet may be used.

You can also purchase complete wood-graining kits. These kits generally contain a wood-graining tool such as a sponge or the manufacturer's special wood-graining tool. If buying a kit, always read through the manufacturer's instructions completely before beginning.

You should practice graining procedures on a scrap piece of wood before actual application.

Graining should be applied in random patterns, running the full length of the surface. Do not stop in the middle. Various grain effects may be produced by varying the pressure applied or by slightly turning your wrist during the stroke.

1.   Apply antique base coat. Page 62.

2.   Apply colored antique glaze. Page 63.

Do not remove all the glaze from surface. If too much glaze is removed from surface, add more glaze.

Keep graining tool from becoming saturated with glaze. A clean graining tool will produce a better pattern.

3.   Using the selected graining tool, draw it across surface.

4.   Stop at the end of a stroke only. Check surface frequently for desired results.

SPATTERING

Spattering is a technique used in decorating to simulate normal wear and age. It is often combined with highlighting effects. Page 66.

Spattering is usually applied with a stiff-bristle brush, such as a toothbrush. The best results are achieved with darker colors, such as flat black paint, ink, or antiquing glaze. Sometimes, a combination of several bright colors, blue, green, or yellow, are effectively used for an interesting effect. As with most decorating effects, it is recommended that you test your colors and procedures on a scrap piece of wood first.

Be sure surface is thoroughly dry before beginning the spattering. The spatter pattern can be controlled in several ways. One way is to knock a brush against a stick held about 6 to 10 inches from the surface.

1. Dip brush in paint. Aim at desired area of surface. Strike brush against stick.

2. After spattering is dry, apply a clear finish.

MARBLEIZING

Marbleizing is the name of the method used to simulate marble on a glass or wood surface. Authentic marble is made up of many colors, with base colors such as white, cream, pink, and black. They are often mixed with other colors to produce interesting shades and effects.

You should take a color photograph of a suitable piece of marble and use it as a guide when marbleizing. Usually two other colors are used with the base coat. In addition, black is often used for accenting.

Oil-based paints should be used for marbleizing as well as for the base coat. Be sure the surface is properly sanded and sealed before beginning.

1. Apply base coat. Page 62. Allow to dry until tacky.

2. Using artist's brush or small stick, apply one color [1] in an uneven dribble pattern.

In succeeding colors, apply only about one-half the amount of paint used in Step 2.

3. Repeat Step 2 with additional colors [2] as desired.

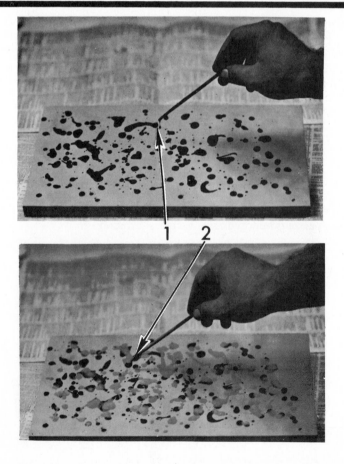

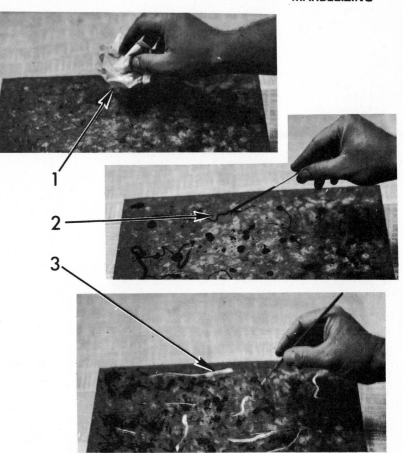

4. Using a crumpled paper [1], pat the surface lightly, following the basic pattern of the colors.

Be sure to change paper occasionally when it becomes saturated with paint.

5. Continue patting surface [1] and edges until desired effect is obtained.

6. Using a stick, apply small amounts of black across surface [2] in a random pattern. Lightly pat these areas with crumpled paper.

For a more realistic effect, veins may be added in thin, uneven lines.

7. Using a stick or thin artist's brush and white paint, apply veins [3] to surface.

8. Allow surface to dry thoroughly.

9. Apply a clear, semigloss finish. Page 36.

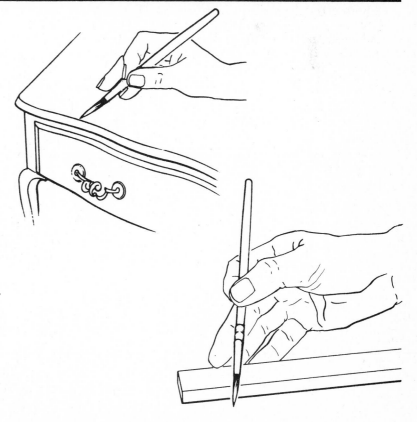

▰▰▰ STRIPING ▰▰▰

Striping is a technique used to accent edges or carvings by painting a thin line on these surfaces. Usually a contrasting color is used. Metallic paints such as gold or silver are often used. An artist's brush is most often used for application.

Before striping, be sure the surface is free of dirt and wax.

1. Dip brush into paint to depth of bristles. Draw brush out against edge of container to remove excess paint.

To guide your hand when striping, run your third and fourth fingers along the edge of the surface. If striping is applied too far from edge of surface, have someone hold a straightedge in place as the guide. Take your time. Apply a few practice strokes to a piece of scrap before each application.

2. With paint remaining in brush after practice strokes, apply striping to desired surface.

3. Repeat Steps 1 and 2 until surface has been completed.

Decaling a piece of furniture is an easy way to brighten an item at low cost with little effort. Decals are used to simulate intricate patterns such as striping or stenciling. Some decals have a hand-painted look, complete with brush strokes.

There is a great variety of decals—everything from landscapes and ships to flowers, letters, and numbers. They are available in many sizes.

Decals may generally be found in arts and crafts stores or home improvement centers. They can be applied to almost any surface. Decals may be used as an accent to other decorating effects such as antiquing or graining.

Before applying decals, be sure the surface is free of dust, dirt, and grease. Be sure freshly painted surfaces are completely dry.

1. Place decal [1] in warm water for about 15 seconds.

2. Remove decal [1] from water. Allow decal to stand for about one minute.

Be sure to position decal correctly the first time. It is difficult to reposition a decal without damaging it.

3. Position decal directly above desired placement.

4. While holding decal [2] in position, carefully slide backing [3] from decal.

5. Using a soft cloth, carefully smooth decal [4] by lightly wiping from center to outer edges.

6. Allow decal to dry thoroughly before touching.

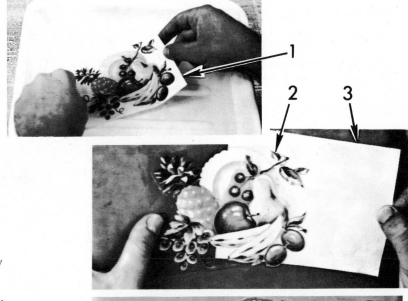

Decoupage is the technique of applying a print or design to a surface, then giving it the appearance of being part of the surface by applying many coats of a clear finish to the surface. Almost any flat or almost flat item may be used. Some of the commonly used items are pictures, sketches, photographs, or greeting cards.

Decoupage may be applied over a clear or colored finish. When antiquing, the print may be applied under the glaze or over the glaze before the clear finish is applied. Always consider your final, clear top coat finish when selecting the undercoat. Most manufacturers will recommend a top coat that is compatible with their product. As a rule, enamels and enamel undercoats are used under varnishes; latex, vinyl stains, and acrylics under lacquers.

Varnish is the most frequently used clear finish. The traditional finish is applied in 40 coats. However, the number of applications depends on the desired effect.

There are new synthetic finishes available, such as polymer resin. These synthetic finishes are simply poured on and give the appearance of about 40 coats of varnish.

There are several ways to prepare prints for decoupage to achieve different effects. One of the more often used methods is to cut out the entire print [1], although the print with background is also used occasionally.

When selecting a print to cut out, select one that is not too detailed. A simple print that has been neatly cut looks better than a poorly cut, detailed print.

Another method is to tear out the print [2], leaving an uneven edge. There will also be a white edge of paper around the border if it is torn toward you.

A burned edge may be produced with a small candle, match, or lighter. Hold the print [3] face up and level as you pass the edges of the print over the flame. As soon as the paper catches fire, blow it out. Continue going around the edges until the desired effect is obtained. A more uniform and controlled burn can be made by rolling the print and burning the rolled ends.

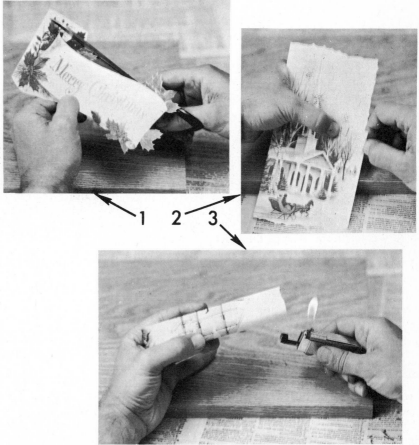

1 2 3

DECOUPAGE

The following tools and supplies are required to decoupage:

Small scissors [1], if required
Varnish brush [2] with chiseled edge
Small brush [3], used for spreading glue
Hard rubber roller [4] or rolling pin
Sanding block [5]
Razor blade, if required to remove air bubbles from print.
Sandpaper, 400 grade
Extra fine grade finishing pads or steel wool, 000 or 0000 grade
White glue
Decoupage sealer, aerosol or liquid
Clear finish
Wax paper
Clean, lint-free cloth
Print, as desired

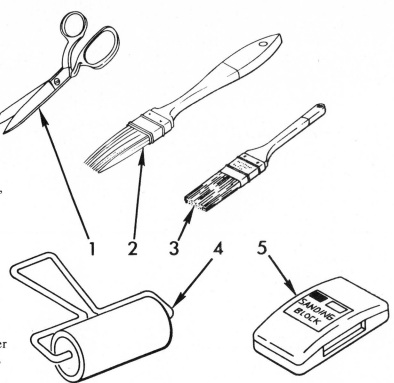

Manufacturers are constantly introducing new products that last longer, act both as an adhesive and finish, are easier to apply and result in thicker coats. Because of these continual improvements, these procedures should be used only as a guide.

It is recommended that bare wood be sealed with a clear finish before decoupage. Be sure surface is free of dirt and sanding dust before applying print.

1. Carefully cut, tear, or burn print [1] to desired size.

2. Place print [1] face up on wax paper.

A light coat of decoupage sealer should be applied to both sides of the print. This will prevent the colors from bleeding through and will also strengthen the print.

If decoupage sealer is applied with a brush, it should be applied with a single stroke in one direction. Do not brush back and forth. This may cause the colors to run.

3. Apply a light coat to print [1]. Allow to dry according to manufacturer's instructions.

4. Turn print [1] over. Repeat Step 3.

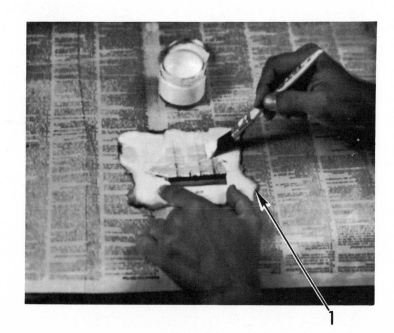

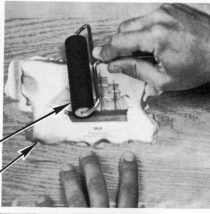

5. Hold print against surface at desired location. Lightly mark outline of print [1].

6. Remove print [1]. Place print face down on wax paper.

7. Spread glue evenly over back of print [3].

8. Place print [3] in desired position as marked in Step 5.

9. Place clean wax paper over print [3]. Using roller [2], press firmly over print to remove excess glue and air bubbles.

10. Remove wax paper. Using damp cloth [4], remove excess glue from edges of print.

11. Repeat Steps 9 and 10 until no glue appears around edges of print.

12. Allow glue to dry overnight.

The surface is now ready for the finish. Go to pages as indicated for type of finish you have selected:

- Synthetic finish — Page 36.
- Antiquing glaze — Page 63.
- Varnish — Go to Page 36 for instructions for applying varnish before continuing with this page.

Sanding will be required at some point before the last coat to remove any rough or high spots.

13. Before sanding, apply at least six coats of varnish to entire surface [1].

14. Using sanding block and sandpaper, lightly sand entire surface [2]. Wipe clean with dry cloth.

15. Apply additional coats of varnish until desired effect is achieved. After final coat has been applied, allow surface to dry thoroughly.

16. Using finishing pad or steel wool, rub surface [2] lightly for a smooth satin finish.

17. Apply a coat of furniture wax.

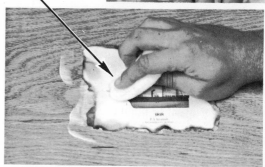

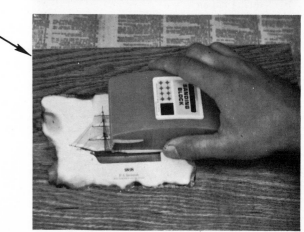

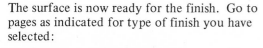

Stenciling is a technique that is frequently used to decorate furniture. It can be used to:

- Transfer a design from one item to another. For example, if you have a chair with an attractive design painted on it, you may wish to reproduce it on another chair, table, or other item.

- Apply the same design to several items. You may wish to decorate a group of items, for example a set of kitchen chairs, so that they match. Stenciling provides the means for applying identical designs to any number of items.

It is possible to create your own designs or reproduce designs that you find on other furniture, in children's color books, in magazines, or many other sources. For most of us, it is best that the design be exactly the same size that we wish to use on the item.

If you wish to make a large or complex design, you may find it easier to build it up from several smaller stencils. By using several stencils, you can create as intricate a design as you wish.

If you wish to use several colors in a design, you have two methods available:

- Prepare a separate stencil for each color. This method is particularly applicable if the design consists of distinct areas of color and you wish to use aerosol paint.

- Apply the entire design with one color. Then paint the different parts of the design with the different colors. This method is best if the design consists basically of one color and requires only highlighting or other limited decorating.

This section describes how to do the different operations required to stencil. They are:

Cutting Stencils, below.
Applying Stencils, Page 76.
Decorating Stencils, Page 77.

With these techniques you can create interesting decorating effects. They can be combined effectively with other techniques such as Antiquing, Page 54.

▶ **Cutting Stencils**

The following tools and supplies are required:

Sharp knife [1]
Small scissors [2]
Stencil paper or architect's linen. These materials are available at craft shops. Stiff paper such as used in manila folders is suitable for making a stencil if it will not be used many times.
Carbon paper
Tracing paper
Masking tape
Scotch tape. Use for repairing stencil.
Black or dark-colored paper
Soft lead pencil. No. 2 lead
Sandpaper, 220 Grade extra fine

Several smaller stencils may be used to build up a larger, more intricate design. Number of stencils to use in applying a design must be determined.

1. Using pencil and tracing paper, trace design [3].

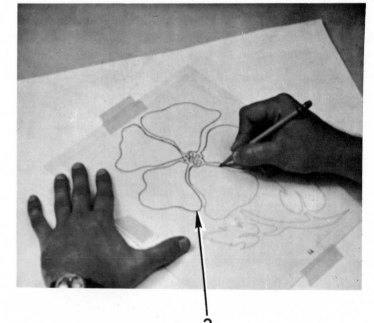

Cutting Stencils

2. Place carbon paper on stencil paper.

3. Place tracing paper over carbon paper.

4. Using masking tape, fasten tracing paper and carbon paper to stencil paper.

5. Using sharp pencil, trace design [1] through carbon paper onto stencil paper.

6. Check that design has been transferred to stencil paper. Leave one end of tracing paper fastened to stencil paper so that you do not loose its position.

If design is incomplete, continue tracing. Be sure that tracing paper is in correct position on stencil paper.

If design is complete, go to Step 7.

7. Remove tracing paper and carbon paper [2].

8. Using pencil, shade in all areas to be cut out from stencil paper.

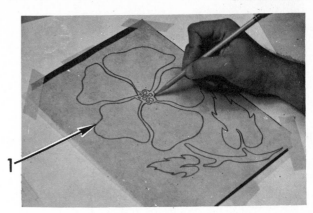

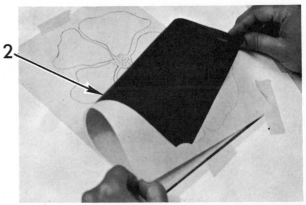

Cutting Stencils

Some designs require that connecting strips [1] of stencil paper be left to hold parts of the design together. The spaces left in the design by the connecting strips may be painted later.

9. Draw connecting strips, as required.

10. Carefully cut out each section [2] of the design. Be sure not to cut through connecting strips. If a connecting strip is cut, tape it together with Scotch tape.

11. Check back of stencil for rough edges. Sand lightly, as required, to smooth edges.

12. Place stencil on dark paper [3]. Check that all edges of cutouts are smooth. There must be no burrs or frayed edges.

13. Apply stencil. Page 76.

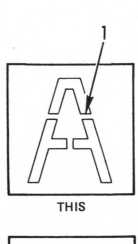

THIS

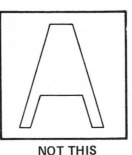

NOT THIS

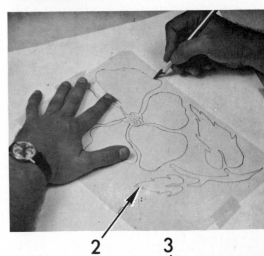

STENCILING

▶ Applying Stencils

The following tools and supplies are required:

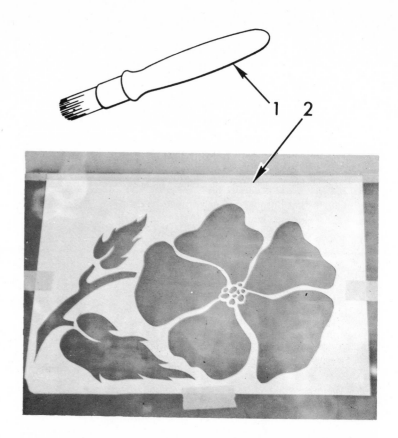

> Stencil brush [1], if desired. A stencil brush is held perpendicular to the work surface. Paint is applied by tapping the bristles onto the design. Do not use a brushing or stroking motion with a stencil brush.
>
> Stencil [2]
>
> Paint. Aerosol spray paint may be used instead of fluid paints and stencil brush.
>
> Varnish, if desired. Varnish may be used to hold stencil to surface so that paint does not run under edges of cutouts. If varnish is used to hold stencil, stencil must be made of stencil paper or architect's linen. Varnish is applied to surface. After it becomes tacky, stencil is placed on varnish. If aerosol spray paint is used, stencil may be fastened to surface with masking tape only.
>
> Extra fine grade finishing pads, 220 grade sandpaper or No. 000 steel wool

Surface must be clean and dry.

1. Fasten stencil [2] to surface. Be sure that stencil is in correct location on surface.

Applying Stencils

2. Check that:

   > Stencil is located correctly on surface.
   > Edges of cutouts are against surface.

If applying paint with stencil brush, be sure to:

- Place work surface in horizontal position.
- Remove excess paint from bristles by tapping them against scrap paper.
- Hold brush perpendicular to surface.
- Apply paint by tapping rather than brushing.
- Work from edges to center of cutout.

If applying paint with aerosol spray, be sure to mask surface and work area thoroughly. Read Applying Aerosol Finishes, Page 48.

3. Apply paint.

If aerosol spray is used, different effects may be obtained by applying paint lightly [1] or more heavily [2].

4. Allow paint to dry.

5. Decorate stencil design as desired. Page 77.

► **Decorating Stencils**

A stencil can be made more attractive with the addition of detail work. Adding colors, painting leaf ribs, and highlighting rounded surfaces with paint or metallic powders are examples of decorating stencils.

► **Applying Detail to Stencils**

A fine-tipped artist's brush [1] is best for adding fine lines and applying paint to small areas.

1. Apply detail, as desired.

2. Allow paint to dry.

If gold or bronze highlights are desired, go to next section (below) for Applying Metallic Powder.

If stencil is completed but additional protection of stencil is desired, apply varnish. Page 36.

► **Applying Metallic Powder to Stencils**

Gold or bronze highlights are frequently used to help provide a rounded appearance to objects such as grapes or other fruit common to stencil designs. These highlights can be obtained by the use of metallic powders.

The following tools and supplies are required:

    Brush [1] for applying varnish
    Stencil
    Piece of velvet. Used to apply metallic
        powder.
    Clean, lint-free cloth
    Varnish
    Metallic powder
    Extra fine grade finishing pads, 220 Grade
        extra fine sandpaper, or No. 000 steel
        wool

1. Apply varnish to surface. Varnish may be thinned with thinner before applying.

2. Allow varnish to dry until tacky. Varnish can be tested to determine correct tackiness as follows:

Carefully touch your knuckles to surface. While removing knuckles from surface, you should feel a slight pull.

If surface is not dry enough, stencil will stick to surface, leaving marks when removed.

If surface is too dry, powder will not stick to surface. If varnish is too dry, allow it to dry 24 hours. Then apply more varnish.

3. Place stencil on surface.

4. Check that:

    Stencil is located correctly on surface.
    Edges of cutouts are against surface.

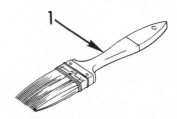

Applying Metallic Powder to Stencils

In next step, a piece of velvet (pile side out) will be used to pick up the powder and apply it to the surface.

5. Using velvet, apply powder to a scrap of dark paper or wood with tapping motion to become familiar with this technique.

Usually, powder is applied in heavier concentration near the edges of cutouts. If rounded subjects, such as fruit, are being stenciled, the powder is applied to the outer edges and moved with curved strokes toward the middle. This will give an appearance of roundness.

On larger rounded subjects, lighter colored powder may be used to highlight selected areas.

6. Apply powder to design [1].

Applying Metallic Powder to Stencils

Be sure to use a circular motion, and polish as you rub powder over the stencil. This will ensure a permanent contact with varnished surface.

7. Rub powder over cutouts in stencil. Apply powder from outside edges of each cutout toward the center.

8. After stencil design is completed, carefully lift stencil from varnished surface. Do not spill excess powder from stencil onto tacky varnish.

9. Allow varnish to dry thoroughly.

10. Using damp cloth, wipe stenciled design to remove excess powder. You may be able to turn item over and tap back surface to knock off excess powder.

11. Apply varnish to surface. Allow to dry.

12. Apply another coat of varnish to surface. Allow to dry.

13. Using finishing pad, sandpaper, or steel wool, lightly sand surface.

14. Apply satin-finish varnish, if desired.

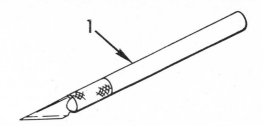

Beautiful and intricate inlay designs can be made using common household items and clear varnish.

These procedures should be used as guidelines for creating simulated inlay designs.

The following tools and supplies are required to apply simulated inlay designs:

> Sharp knife [1] or razor blade
> Masking tape, 2-inch width
> Bleach, if desired
> Wood stain
> Clear varnish
> Selected inlay pattern design or stencil

If a dark inlay design is desired, do not bleach surface. Surface should be stained.

1. Stain or bleach entire surface as required. See Applying Stains, Page 33, or Bleaching, Page 25.

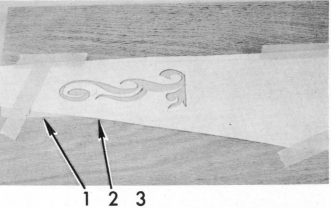

2. Locate and mark exact area where inlay design is to be placed.

3. Cover this marked area with 2-inch masking tape [1].

4. Position stencil [2] or inlay pattern over masked area. Tape stencil or pattern in position.

If using inlay patterns, cut must be made completely through pattern and tape. Be sure to make cut edges as clean, sharp, and crisp as possible.

CAUTION

When cutting through tape, be careful not to cut deeply into surface.

5. Using sharp knife or razor blade, carefully cut design [3] through tape.

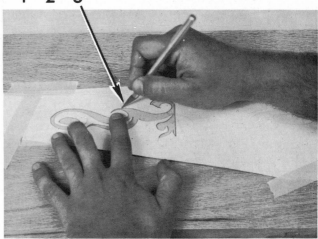

SIMULATED INLAY

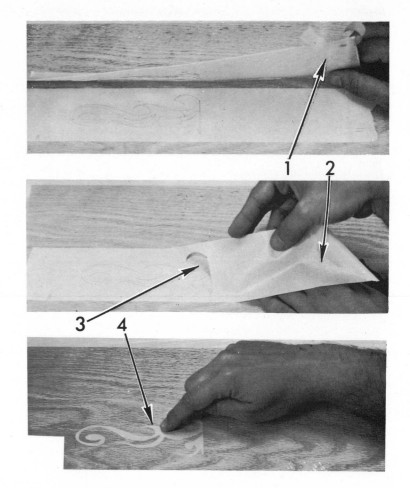

6. Carefully remove stencil [1] or pattern.

When removing excess tape [2], be sure it is completely separated from inlay pattern tape [3].

7. Carefully remove excess tape [2].

8. Check that the edges of inlay pattern tape [4] are sharp and crisp.

If edges are not sharp and crisp, design will be fuzzy and appear to bleed after staining. Recut edges of tape inlay as necessary.

9. Press down all edges of inlay pattern tape [4] smoothly and firmly.

10. Carefully apply desired wood stain to entire surface. Page 33.

11. After wiping wood stain, remove masking tape inlay design [1].

You should now have a sharp, crisp simulated inlay design.

If additional separation between design and background is desired, you should use a very fine-tipped pen and add black ink to outline the design.

If additional color is desired, colored felt-tipped pens may be used to color the design.

12. Apply a clear varnish or clear synthetic finish to protect entire surface. Go to Page 36 for Applying Clear Finish.

Distressing is another technique used to add the antique or aged appearance and simulate wear. Distressing techniques may be applied at any time before application of the final coat. Distressing may also be combined with other decorating effects such as graining or spattering.

There are many and varied methods for distressing. Some of the more common distressing techniques are:

- Holes made with nails, ice picks, drill bits, etc.

- Dents made with stones, chains, or ballpeen hammer

- Rounded edges and heavy-wear areas made with files and rasps

- Burning or charring

Usually all distressing effects should be sanded to give a natural, time-worn appearance.

Three of the more common techniques are described in this section: worn edges, burning, and worm holes.

- Worn Edges. Worn or rounded edges are probably the most obvious signs of age on a piece of furniture. If you want to give a worn look to a new piece of furniture, you should round off sharp edges with a file or a rasp. Before rounding the edges you should attempt to find a similar object and observe the areas that are worn down. Kinds and locations of wear are:

    Around edges [1] of table top or drawer
    One edge or corner [2] worn more than
      others
    Scratches, dents or cuts along a worn edge
      or leg [3]
    Front chair rungs or stretchers [4] between
      table legs

After rounding the edges, they may be sanded smooth or left with a slightly rough appearance.

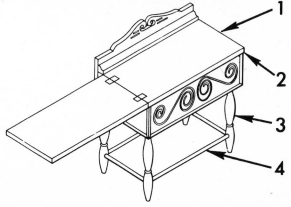

DISTRESSING

• Burning. Finishes often darken with age around corners and in crevices. Burning is usually more effective than staining these areas to achieve this look. A propane torch [1] is the best tool to use when irregularly darkening wood in corners and crevices.

The darkened area may or may not be cleaned with a wire brush [2]. A wire brush can be used to remove the charred wood and emphasize the wood grain in contrast to the surrounding charred finish. After removing the charred wood with a wire brush, polish the area with steel wool [3]. Either a clear finish or a paste wax should be applied.

• Worm Holes. One of the best ways to produce worm holes is with an ice pick, small drill bits, or small, tapered nails. Keep in mind that worms are not the same size and the holes that they bore are also not the same size and that there is no specific pattern. Generally, holes are found in only the softer parts of the wood in a piece of furniture.

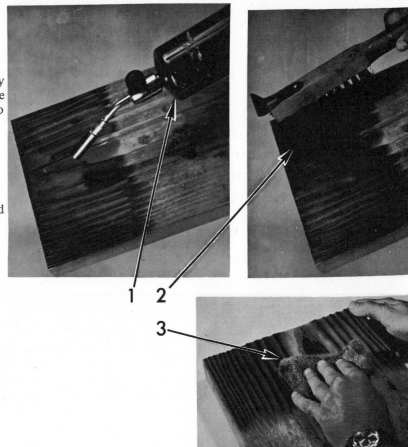

PROJECT	DATE	FINISH	MATERIAL
PROJECT	DATE	FINISH	MATERIAL

PROJECT	DATE	FINISH	MATERIAL

PROJECT	DATE	FINISH	MATERIAL

PROJECT	DATE	FINISH	MATERIAL

PROJECT	DATE	FINISH	MATERIAL

PROJECT	DATE	FINISH	MATERIAL

PROJECT	DATE	FINISH	MATERIAL

PROJECT	DATE	FINISH	MATERIAL

PROJECT	DATE	FINISH	MATERIAL

PROJECT	DATE	FINISH	MATERIAL

NOTES

NOTES

NOTES

NOTES

NOTES

NOTES

NOTES

NOTES